The *real* Book On
HOW TO COOK

Secrets mother never told you

Faith Knight

Published by
Perry Harris Publishing LLC

The Real Book on How to Cook
Secrets mother never told you

Published by:
Perry Harris Publishing

Cover Photos: Wavebreak Media Ltd., Dreamstime.com | Gosphotodesign, Bigstock.com | IS2, Bigstock.com | Leaf, Bigstock.com | monkeybusinessimages, Dreamstime.com

Interior Images: flippo, Bigstock.com | Nsmphoto, Dreamstime.com | Otna Ydur, Bigstock.com | morgan1studios, Bigstock.com | design56, Bigstock.com |Redhaze, Bigstock.com | Kateholms, Bigstock.com | grynold, Bigstock.com | elenathewise, Bigstock.com | Konstik, Dreamstime.com | Rob Heiner, Bigstock.com | Karam Miri Photography, Bigstock.com | ViFi, Bigstock.com | margouillat photo, Bigstock.com | bigldesign, Bigstock.com | stvan 4245, Bigstock.com | Dole, Bigstock.com | Yastremska, Bigstock.com | legaa, Bigstock.com

Cover Design: Grafikali Seven

Interior Layout: John Andrews Design

Editing: Kacy Cook

ISBN-13: 978-0-9826190-4-9

Printed in the USA
2nd Edition

This book is in memory of

"Mamas"

Etta Belle Williams and Willie Lee Knight

Acknowledgments

I WOULD like to say thank you to all the women out there who still cook and actually enjoy it. Special thanks to Annette Benson and Sandy Lewis for their contributions to this book.

Moment Of Truth

Every year the Brock family gets together for a meal. Men, women, and children all over the house, and the smell of home-cooked everything is in the air. As is the custom, the men retire to the sun room with their plates to watch sports and talk trash. On this particular day I decided to join them there and the subject of cooking came up, so I began asking the men if they had any tips to share.

The action in that day's game was slow, so I got them to open up—and some enlightening information started flowing. By the time Kenny strolled in, we were knee-deep into the conversation. [Before I go on, you need to know that Kenny is a master at telling a tall tale with a straight face. But he can throw down on the grill so I asked if he had any tips to share]. "Absolutely," he said. Then he proceeded to tell us about his talent for picking up recipes just by watching TV. All he needed to do was watch it once and he had it. So we listened closely while he related *in detail* how to make the best, fried chicken. It sounded really good, even down to the panko he substitutes for flour "to give it that pretty look." We were all taken in. In fact, not a few of the men vowed they would try making *their* chicken that way.

But our newfound knowledge was circumvented when Kenny's wife came in. "Ken has never cooked chicken in his life," she informed us.

Fooled again. But then it hit me: why not write a book – not full of recipes – but rather how to *prepare* them?

That is how this book came about: to share tips and tricks on how to make the time-tested foods prepared by everyday cooks… without any guesswork.

Introduction

We Americans love our relationship with food! Our obsession is pervasive and of course, impossible to avoid because frankly, we all have to eat. But eating *well* is always the goal.

Ever since The Food Network came on the scene, more than 100 million households have spent hours watching its shows: BBQ contests, cupcake contests, master chef contests, and that's not all. Every food category imaginable has a chef connected to it who happily comes into our homes each night to show us their takes on the latest recipes.

We are so enamored of food that we are taking on the cooking shows ourselves, creating our own concoctions. For example, consider the number of food trucks that have sprung up all over the country. According to the National Restaurant Association there are thousands out there rolling around in search of a neighborhood near you.

Manned by new and formerly unknown cooks, these modern-day chuck wagons are turning out creations the cowboy had never dreamed of: salt in ice cream, cake on a stick, or chocolate on a nice juicy steak!

In fact, think of all the cooking apps for the smartphone available these days. They offer everything from daily cupcake recipes to instant videos you can watch as you cook. My iPhone screen is full of them and I still don't have all the ones I really want.

Novice cooks create their own YouTube videos to promote their homegrown-cooking fare. And the bloggers! Remember *Julie & Julia*? Hundreds of people logged onto Julie Powell's site each day to follow her obsession with Julia Child's *Mastering the Art of French Cooking*. Powell's food fetish translated into a book deal and a movie! Yes, our affair with food is even communal. But the reasons go beyond just our love of food.

A recent survey conducted by Harris Interactive found that 4 out of 5 Americans say they are spending 5-6 days a week cooking at home. That's almost equivalent to the norms of the 1950s – when fast food was practically unheard of. There are several reasons for this resurgence.

Cooking at home means we retain more of the nutritional value in our food, not to mention fewer artificial flavors and colors. Americans are also paying more attention to their health as conditions like obesity and diabetes proliferate. Even concerns over food safety factor in. But one of the biggest attractions to home cooking is the view of it as recreation. And although we haven't given up eating out altogether, there is definitely a trend emerging in the area of DIY dining.

So once you have acquired all your recipes on your tablet and watched so much Bobby Flay that you could OD, it's time to focus on your approach. You can't just buy a bunch of ingredients, bring them home and think you are going to whip up the next blue-ribbon recipe. First you need to understand the method behind the mastery.

Most recipe books, apps and videos have little time to show you the ropes; the real nuts and bolts, the "meat and potatoes" of what goes into cooking. But never fear, you've come to right place. *The Real Book on*

How to Cook will give you the background information you need to help build your confidence as you tackle a slew of new recipes.

I started cooking when I was 12 and picked up things here and there from family as well as friends, and over the years, the most important lesson I learned about food was that good cooking has an order that must be followed.

Now that I am also a project manager, I go about everything with the same attention to order. That's how I came up with "POTS"—not cooking pots, but P.O.T.S., which stands for **P**reparation, **O**rganization, and **T**echnique, equals **S**uccess. This book is structured on the POTS strategy I developed, as I became a more proficient cook. Once you are cookin' in the kitchen, you will be able to easily adapt my strategy to make it your own, that is, if you are determined to be a good cook.

With the help of this book, you are going to learn to cook the way Mama always did. Not by copying her recipes or donning her apron, but by learning the hidden tips she knew but never told you. She didn't withhold these intentionally. The truth is most good cooks "just do it" and cannot articulate step-by-step instructions. They have been doing it for so long that it has become second nature to them. Stopping to think about how they do it, let alone trying to pass on those tips, becomes overwhelming. I know this because I interviewed a dozen home cooks and tried to get them to tell me their secrets. Even they were amazed at the number of steps they "just do" without thinking. As I questioned these cooks, I had to stop them several times to point out just how much they were leaving out of their instructions! The process was complex, but the results were fabulous.

In this book you will learn tips, tricks, and techniques cooks have used for generations to make those scrumptious Sunday dinners we all remember from our childhoods. The information in this book will teach you all you need to know to become more comfortable with cooking and to prepare delicious homemade meals.

This is not your typical cookbook; rather, it supplies the practical details every cook needs to pull off even the most challenging recipes. Actually, the term *cookbook* is a misnomer. Most cookbooks don't teach you how to cook; they provide recipes and assume you already know the basics. My goal is to tell you what most cookbooks don't.

As all good cooks know, cooking goes way beyond just throwing some items into a bowl. You must understand the ingredients—how they are used, how you should handle them, and what preparation is necessary to use them effectively. Those steps are often left out by the chef on your favorite cooking show. They make it look so easy. But what you don't see is much of the prep work needed to get those ingredients to play nice together.

One of the most important things all good cooks understand is timing. For instance, cookbooks do not usually tell you whether one of your ingredients can sit on the counter before it is added or if it must remain refrigerated. Many may not offer details about what something should look like once you've beaten it on medium speed, or even what "medium" means. Just these two bits of information can make the difference between a successful meal and a disaster. The lack of such knowledge is one of the chief reasons that cookbooks end up on a dusty shelf, never to be used again.

The Real Book on How to Cook is designed to prepare you for obstacles you will likely face while tackling a recipe. The first thing you will learn is the importance of **Preparation** before you begin cooking. The prerequisites are few, but they are important and will make for a much better experience if followed. Next we will take the time to help you get to know your surroundings and show you how to make the most of your kitchen type. You will learn how to get into the cooking "zone."

We'll focus on the **Organization** of your cooking project by examining the tools that make it all happen. You'll learn about the types of cookware and utensils you will need and their uses.

Technique is crucial to creating a memorable dish. In this chapter, you will get to know your ingredients and how to skillfully choose and handle them. What goes well with what? Pay close attention to these tips because these are the gems your mother never told you!

The **Success** section pulls it all together with how-to examples you can try right now. These step-by-step instructions will help you to effectively prepare some of the most common foods cooked in kitchens today. I've even answered some of your cooking questions in the **Cooking FAQs** section.

You will also find advice on how to get the most from your recipe source, whether it is a cookbook, a cooking show or a meal your friend makes that you would like to try.

To ensure you understand all the time-tested secrets offered, you will be quizzed at the end of each chapter. You can find all the answers in the **Appendix**. You will also notice ample white space to jot down notes about the things you learn on your cooking journey. Take advantage of these areas throughout the book.

You're ready for a challenge, right? As the saying goes, if you can't stand the heat, get out of the kitchen!

Now let's get started!

Table Of Contents

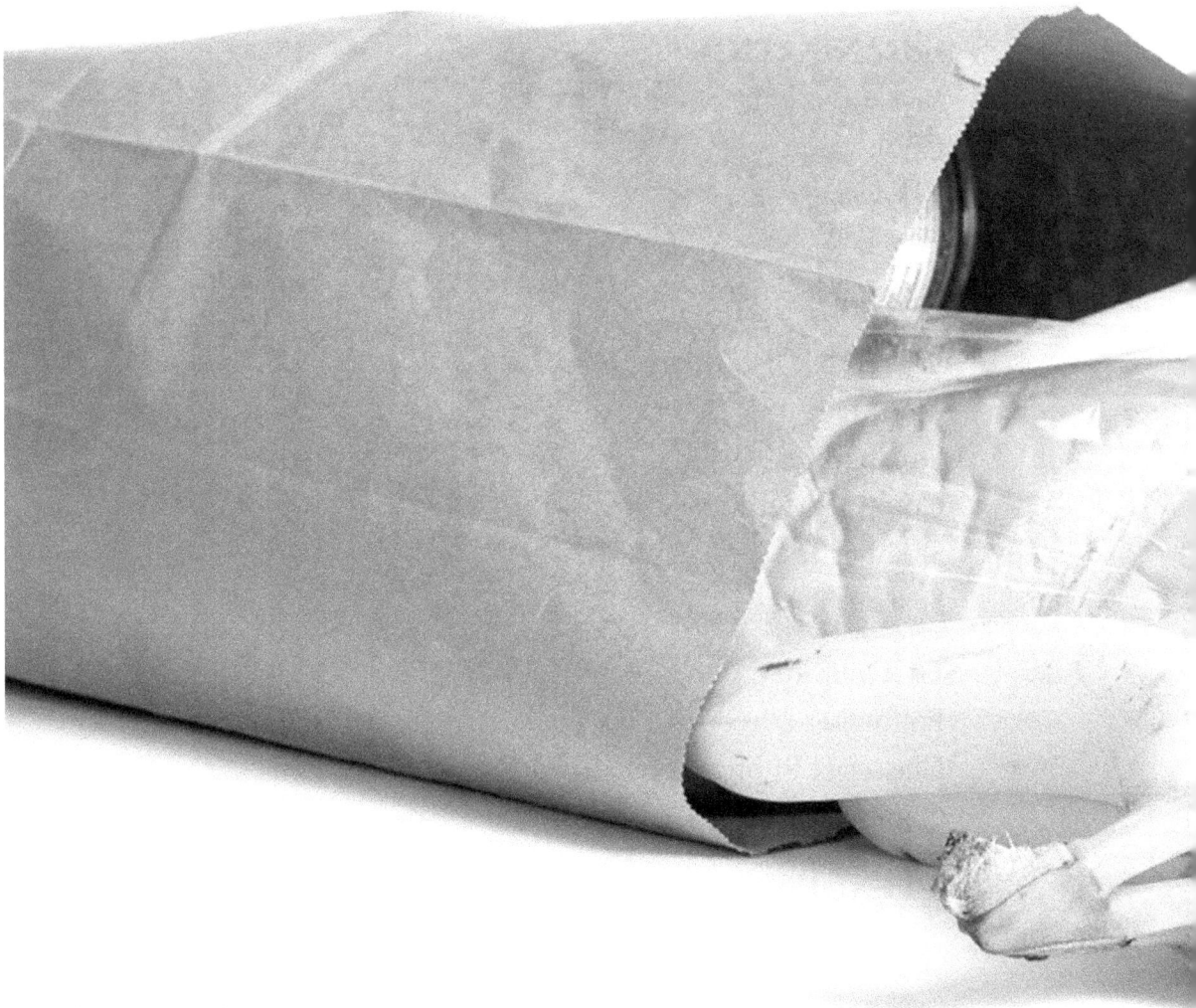

Preparation

- Hygiene
- Environment
- Ambiance
- Consumers

"My mother gave me a real kick toward cooking,
which was that if I wanted to eat,
I'd better know how to do it myself. "

—*Daniel Craig*

Hygiene

When I am about to cook a meal for family or friends, I cannot get started until two conditions are met: 1) the kitchen is clean and 2) my hands are clean.

As you become more proficient, you will begin to discover certain pet peeves that have the potential to ruin your cooking mood. For me, a clean kitchen is a feel-good kind of thing. There's something about clean dishes, a cleared counter and stovetop that puts me in a much better mood to cook. However, there is also a practical argument for a clean kitchen: less mess. It's easier to know where everything is when you are starting from scratch rather than adding more disorder to an already chaotic situation.

Wash the dishes beforehand and put them away. Wipe down the counters with antibacterial spray to ensure you don't start off adding insult to injury with germs as the main course.

Clean floors are also nice, though not a must since you are not cooking on the floor. I trust you will not be dropping food there and reusing it.

The second condition that must be met before getting started is clean hands. Never cook anything without clean hands. In fact, washing your hands throughout the cooking process is a great habit to get into. Here are **three** good reasons why:

1. **You will be touching "things" then touching food.** Think of your neighborhood sandwich shop. One staff member is supposed to wear gloves to fix the sandwich while another handles the money. However, I have seen one worker doing both—and without gloves. Touching things and then touching food spreads germs. Would you eat that sandwich after seeing him do that? No. Your family and friends don't want to eat germs either.

2. **You may be handling formerly live animals.** This may freak you out, but keep in mind that some of the things we cook used to breathe, walk, crawl and swim before they ended up in our refrigerators. These now-dead creatures may still be carrying infections and viruses that will only disappear during the cooking process, so before you cook these you should take steps to protect yourself and your clean kitchen. For instance, be especially careful when handling raw chicken. It is very germy. I suggest wearing some cooking gloves – you can get some cheap ones by the pack in the cleaning supply aisle at the grocery. Wear them when you cut up the chicken as well as when you take it out of the packaging and transfer it to a pan, pot, or bowl. Even if you plan to store it in a freezer bag or aluminum foil, you should wear gloves. You may think wearing gloves is overkill, but we're not grabbing chickens from the backyard and chopping off their heads like your ancestors used to do. These days, you don't know where that bird has been! But if you insist on handling it with your bare hands, DO NOT touch anything else until you wash them with warm, soapy water.

3. **You will eventually stick your finger in your mouth.** Everyone who has ever cooked anything has tasted it. Even if you are unconsciously attempting to get some sauce off your fingers, the first place they end up is in your mouth. It's inevitable. During that momentary lapse in judgment, you will not remember that you just touched that germy chicken, or that someone else is going to eat the sauce you just stuck your finger in to see if it needed salt. If you must taste as you cook (and you must) here is the best method: set aside a separate spoon just for tasting and use that spoon to put a little of the food in a small bowl, cup or plate, and then dip your finger in that. This method allows you to reuse the spoon without contaminating the food.

The most important thing to remember is to make it a habit to wash your hands before, during, and after the cooking process.

Once you are ready to cook, here is a tip that can help: If you are cutting onions or peeling potatoes, create a mini-garbage dump. To do this, get a plastic grocery bag and a plastic bowl; the bowl should be large enough to hold about 5 cups of anything. Line the bowl with the plastic bag as if lining a kitchen trash can. Set this bowl on one of the kitchen counters near where you are cutting so that you can toss in onion and potato skins as well as used paper towels, meat trimmings, or the inedible parts of vegetables. Once you are done with this work you can simply pick up the bag, tie it, toss it in the trashcan and—voilà!— instant cleanup.

Personal Cleanliness

You may recall the cafeteria ladies from your days in grade school. Some were lovable and treated you like their children, while others were hard and tough with looks that could kill. But one thing they all had in common was a hairnet. These nets served a purpose: hair is not a condiment, and therefore has no place in the kitchen where it can get into food and subsequently into the mouths of those who eat it.

If you have relatively long hair, or hair that is prone to breakage, you really should wear a net when you cook. For example, I have very long hair and I sometimes notice I've left strands of it behind—in the bathroom, of course, but I've also found it on countertops. Once I even found a strand in my refrigerator! Yuk is right! So I am very conscious about where my hair is when I'm cooking; it's usually tied up in a bun or under a net. I'd advise you to do likewise. If you don't wear a net or some kind of scarf on your head, resist the urge to touch your hair. Some people have a hair fetish, and they can't keep their hands out of it. They are constantly rolling strands around their finger, stroking or patting it. If this sounds like you, you MUST wear a net or scarf or else you will end up putting all your hairy germs in your food. Not good.

Dress the Part

Clothing might seem insignificant when it comes to cooking, but it really is vital to make the right choice of what to wear. Change out of your nice church clothes, for example, because you could get stains on them. Anything that is silk or linen is also bad to wear when cooking. Wearing something you don't really care a lot about is a better choice.

When I cook, I like to wear sweatpants and a T-shirt. The top is loose so I am free to move about, and I don't have to worry about getting anything on it. The pants are just comfortable. I also recommend you get an apron—more than one, in fact. I have four aprons. That way, I can enlist help in the kitchen when I have guests who are so inclined. I don't want to be responsible for ruining somebody's outfit or, worse, having to pay the cleaning bill.

Some people cook in their socks. I even do that every now and then. It's kind of fun to slide from one counter to the other on the tile floor, as long as you are not carrying anything, but I really recommend you wear a pair of sneakers or a pair of sensible shoes while cooking. You could accidentally drop something on your foot and that would not be fun. I own heavy cast iron skillets, ceramic mixing bowls, and very sharp knives so cooking without protecting my feet when using these tools is not an option. By the way, barefoot in the kitchen is just nasty, OK?

Ambiance

Aside from being clean, your kitchen must have the right ambiance. Cooking is a craft and to be successful at it the atmosphere is key. You want your kitchen to be in sync with your personality and the way you work. In short, you need to be at one with it, so it needs to be responsive. How do you get the right balance? One way is to do a major remodel, but who has the time or disposable income to build their dream kitchen? An easier way to do it is to follow two simple suggestions:

#1 Ensure you have breathing room

This means your kitchen needs to be accessible in the areas you'll use most: around the stove, the refrigerator, and the counters. If you are one of those people who bought huge gourmet kitchens but can't boil water, now is the time to take advantage of that goldmine. Having adequate elbowroom allows you to relax and not feel overwhelmed with all the stuff that can pile up during a recipe project.

If you don't have a big shiny kitchen, no worries, just make sure the counters are clutter-free and all the kids' toys are off the floor. As I said earlier, do the dishes. If you don't have a dual sink where you can put them after washing so they can sit and drain, put them away. Just get everything out of the way so you can cook.

#2 Order everyone to hang out elsewhere

People are the number one detriment to good cooking. Have you ever noticed that you never see Jeffrey in the kitchen until Ina Gartner has completed the meal? As a matter of fact, on your favorite cooking shows do you ever see folks running in and out of the kitchen grabbing things? No. Of course, one reason is that they are on TV, but the main reason is they do not want the viewer to be distracted. So why allow people in your kitchen to distract you? The only exception I will grant on this subject is if you have your own TV show with another host to tag team the meal. Don't have your own show? Then there is no reason to have anyone else in the kitchen while you cook (unless you enlist an assistant). By following this suggestion, you will keep your stress level to a minimum. One more thing, this admonition applies to pets too. No matter how much you love your cat or dog, do not, I repeat, do not allow them to jump up on the kitchen table, or the counters or anything else before during or after your meal is prepared. The general rule is to walk into a welcoming atmosphere free of man and beast.

Environment

*E*very kitchen is different. Some are straight and narrow, like the galley kitchen. Others are L-shaped and still others are unusually shaped. Whatever the makeup of your kitchen, take time to get familiar with its flow. If you never cook but only heat things in the microwave, you might want to try this exercise: carry an imaginary pot from your oven to the nearest counter. How many steps is it? Is it too far away? Or is it too close that you might drop the pot by bumping into the counter? Discovering these things before you start cooking will help you better maneuver the room once you get into the cooking zone: that level of concentration that allows no room for error.

If you have a movable island in the center of the kitchen; might it work better somewhere else? For instance, if you know you will be going back and forth from the stove to a wall oven, position the island to allow a clear path between the two. That way you are not bumping into it when you are carrying a roasting pan, or worse, a knife or other instrument. Safety should always be your first priority. We will talk more about that a little later in this chapter.

Counter Surfaces

Another way to get familiar with your layout is to examine the material make up of your countertops. Are they acrylic, stone, or wood?

Each surface type requires different treatment. Let's take some time to get familiar the most popular:

Solid Surface or Acrylic. This material is most well known under a few brand names such as DuPont Corian® and Wilsonart® solid surface, but other companies also make this material. It is non-porous, which means it resists stains. It usually comes in solid colors. It is not as damage-free as granite or quartz, but it is much easier to maintain than laminate. Solid surface can be easily scratched, so you cannot cut directly on the surface. It can also become dull if hard water is allowed to dry on the surface. Lime-Away or CLR ought to help. To keep your counters clean, use warm, soapy water or an ammonia-based household product. Solid surfaces will also melt at 300 degrees or greater, so don't set anything hot on them.

Laminate. This is the countertop material that comes standard in most homes. Its most popular brands are Formica and Wilsonart. Laminate has come a long way since the '60s and can fool you into thinking it's a solid surface or even granite, until you look closely. Beautiful patterns aside, laminate is still easily damaged by cutting directly on the surface, as well as from harsh or abrasive chemicals. Over time you may see it peel up or buckle from water damage or hot items placed on the surface (140 degrees is all it takes). Despite these drawbacks, most people are drawn to its low price, which is why homebuilders install it.

Granite. This surface is the most sought after by gourmet cooks because of its ease of care. It is a hard surface that will not burn or melt if hot items are set directly on it. It also resists scratching. Of all the countertop surfaces on this list, granite is the most expensive. You can clean granite with warm soapy water. Not much else is required.

Quartz. This material is similar to granite in that it is one of the hardest substances in the world. It is non-porous so it never stains, and it comes in a variety of designs. However, unlike granite, it can still be damaged if not cared for properly. You cannot place hot items directly on quartz, but you can cut directly on the surface. Use water and a paper towel or Handi Wipes® for everyday cleaning. For tougher stains Formula 409 on a Scotch-Brite sponge is a good option.

Wood. While it is not the most popular countertop material, some people like the naturalness of wood. The newer wood counters are sealed rather well to resist water damage, and of course they are very beautiful. As you may have already guessed, wood is not resistant to cutting marks or heat. Once or twice a year you may have to renew wood using a specialized oil or wax treatment. Wood counters can also crack and warp if not installed properly. Some butcher-block counters have been known to change shape or move over time!

There are other surfaces out there such as concrete and soapstone, but the ones just mentioned are the most common. Whatever counter type you have or decide to install, check with the manufacturer for how to care for and maintain your counters.

Cutting Boards

Even if your surface is granite, I highly recommend using cutting boards. These come in lots of sizes and materials and are relatively inexpensive. You can get sets of two or three at the local discount store. There are three types that I use in my daily prep routine:

Acrylic. These are dishwasher safe but through use can dull your knives. They are easy to use and lightweight, making them a popular choice for cutting vegetables.

Bamboo. This surface is ideal for preserving the life of your knives, if you take care to preserve its life. Bamboo looks like wood but it's really a plant. It resists discoloration and does not absorb moisture like wood. It is generally stain-resistant too, but if you do see some, using a sponge, rub the board with salt; that should remove them.

Wood. Wood is less likely to dull your knives as acrylic, but it needs more care than the previous two. It gets lots of cuts in it as well and must be sanitized often to prevent cross contamination. It's also the heaviest of the three types.

To preserve wood or bamboo, hand wash with warm sudsy water and dry, then treat with a little walnut or mineral oil once a month. To sanitize, use a vinegar and water solution. If you use your board to cut meat, this should be done after each use.

You might also consider dedicating one board to meats and another to vegetables. Or you can mark one side of a single board with a pen to indicate which side is exclusively for cutting meat.

Safety

A discussion of cutting boards and surfaces would not be complete without a few words about safety, particularly when it comes to using knives.

First, ensure that the knives you use are kept in their proper place. Sets of knives usually come in a block of wood, while individual knives can come in plastic cases or in boxes if they are more expensive. If you don't have a wood block, you can buy knife holders designed to sit inside your utensil drawer. They contain snug plastic that hugs the sides of the knife and keeps it stable.

I recommend washing larger knives by hand, and then drying them with a towel and putting them away. They will stay sharper longer. Some of the best knives, such as Cutco knives, come with a lifetime warranty. These are very, very sharp and so should be handled with extreme care. Other popular brands in the United States are Wusthof and Henckels.

Before you buy knives, ask around. Some are better than others, meaning they can differ in how sharp they are and how easy they are to care for.

All knives should be carefully handled before, during, and after use. Below is a list of some common cooking knives and their uses:

Butcher. This is a common term used for everything from a chef knife to a cleaver. It is smooth edged and is typically used for cutting meat into sections or chopping vegetables. The manufacturer of your

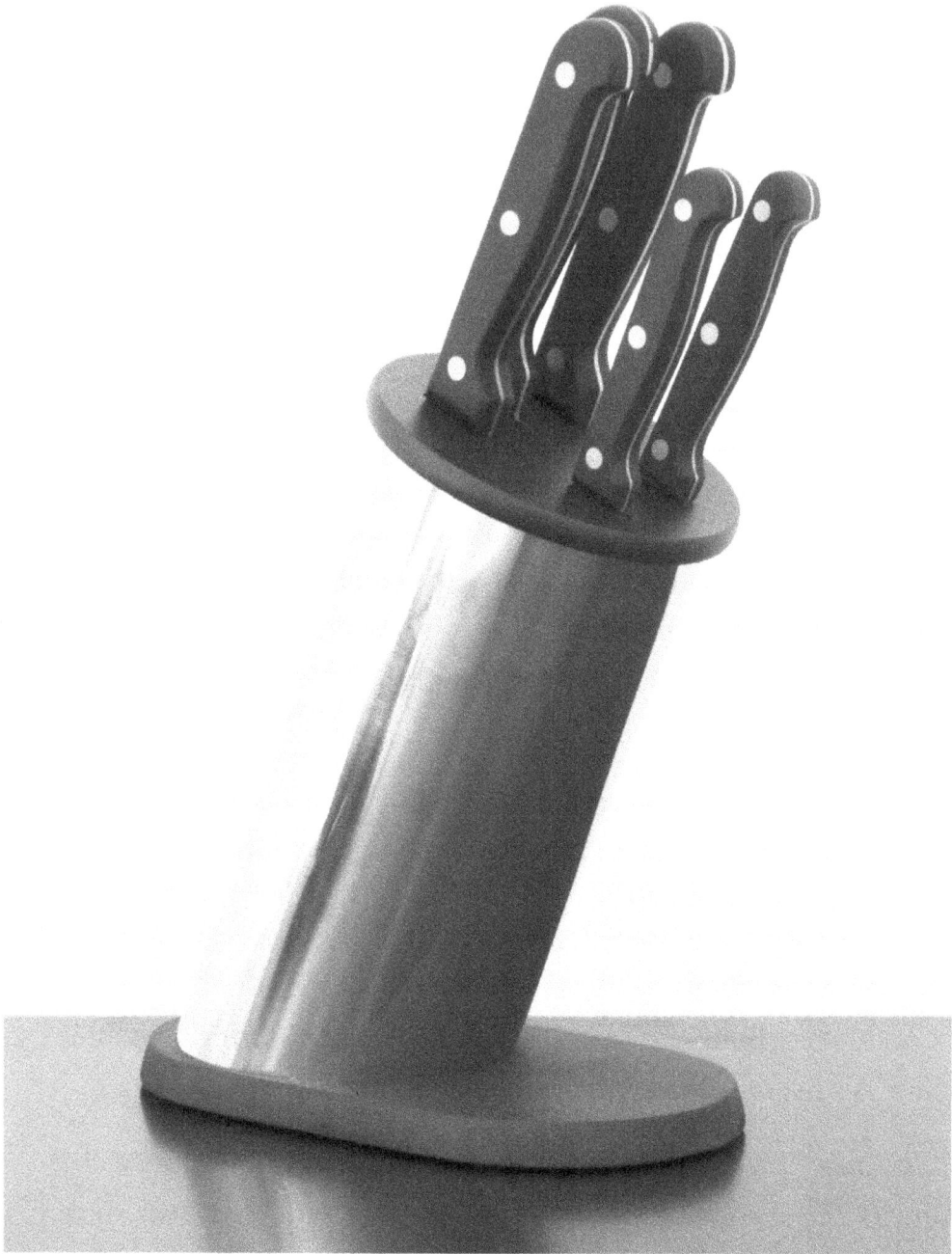

particular knife can tell you its intended use.

Boning. This has a smooth edge and looks like a butcher knife. It is used to cut up chickens and other bone-in meat, but you can use a cleaver to accomplish the same task.

Cleaver. This knife also has a smooth edge but is more square on the ends and is used to debone spare ribs, chickens, etc. It's the knife most butchers use to cut meat.

Serrated. This knife has a jagged edge and is used for cutting crusty bread and other foods that are hard outside but soft inside.

Mama's Tip

That sword-like tool that often comes with a set of knives is NOT for sharpening. It is called a "steel" and is used to keep the edge of the knife in alignment. It's best to have your knives professionally sharpened once a month, if possible.

Paring. This is a short knife used to peel fruits and vegetables.

Never walk around the kitchen carrying a knife; rather, after each use, set it down, and then pick it up again when you need it. There is too much risk of injury in carrying sharp knives around your kitchen.

You must also remember to be careful when handling hot pots and lids. When purchasing new cookware, notice the types of handles and whether they will be heatproof. Some are and some are not. A few of the newer stockpots come with rubber handles and lids with thumb grips so that you do not need potholders. But for most pots, you will need them, so invest in a good pair now. Potholders come as gloves or mitts. Either is fine, depending on your preference. For setting food on your counters, use a trivet or hot pad, which can be wooden or silicone. Always set these out before your food comes out of the oven or off the stove.

Even when checking on your food in the oven or on the stove, do not forget your potholders. Trust me! You don't want to get burned in the middle of a cooking event. It will ruin the rest of the day.

Note: Back in the day, cooks used to use a clothespin to carry hot cake pans from oven to counter. Wonder how they managed that?

Consumers

Depending on what kind of host you are or want to be, keeping your consumer in mind should be of utmost importance. One seasoned cook I know puts a lot of emphasis on presentation. For instance, here are a few questions she suggests you ask yourself when getting ready for your guests:

1) *What type of gathering is it?* A BBQ will require a much different presentation than a formal dinner. This may also determine whether you send invitations or just casually ask guests over.

2) *What kind of crowd is coming?* You want to have a mix of people who will talk to each other and make the event interesting.

3) *What can you prepare in advance?* This is good advice no matter what you are cooking. It will help lessen the amount of stress, as we discussed earlier. In fact, some things taste better the next day—such as spaghetti or chili—so you may want to prepare these in advance.

4) *Know your menu!* You do not want to try something totally new when having an event like this. Familiar is better and will help ensure you do not have a disaster on your hands. Make a to-do list so you don't forget any items.

5) *Clean up the house.* Especially the bathrooms. You want everyone

to feel comfortable and to leave with a good impression. If you can, decorate a little. A tablecloth, place mats, and even place cards are a nice touch.

Another very important thing to determine in advance is whether your guests have any food allergies. You want to find this out before you do any meal planning so that you don't end up killing anyone. I'm serious. There are some things that are inherent in certain foods that can be fatal for those who are allergic. One big one I can think of is peanuts. If you have guests who are allergic to peanuts you might want to ensure your ingredients do not contain them. Another one is wheat. Some people cannot eat anything that contains wheat; foods that don't contain wheat are labeled gluten-free. If someone tells you they cannot eat gluten (pronounced GLUE-ten), they cannot eat wheat products.

Certain preservatives used in salad greens can also be detrimental to people with allergies. Washing greens thoroughly should be a habit, even if the packaging says they are pre-washed. Never take chances. In any event, if you are planning to cook for a mixed company, it's wise to ask in advance about allergies. Most people who have them will inform you, but it doesn't hurt to ask. Some people may not feel comfortable letting you know. Odd as that sounds, it's true.

Here's a little story that illustrates this point:

I have a girlfriend who has a food allergy, which I discovered after the fact. We were at a nightclub that served food during happy hour and was particularly well known for its crab cakes. Not being aware of her allergy, I coaxed her into trying the crab cakes because they were really good. After eating them, her face blew up like a blowfish! I'd never seen anything like it. I rushed her to the nearest hospital and they gave her a shot. Shortly thereafter, she was back to normal. I never understood why she ate the crab cakes in the first place, but ever since then I never take for granted that someone can safely eat something I've prepared. You shouldn't either.

Preparation Quiz

Now it's time to test your understanding of the material previously discussed. Choose the best answer to the question. If you answer the questions correctly, you are ready to move to the next chapter, **Organization**.

1) Before you start to cook, what is the most important thing to do?

a. Turn on the TV in the next room so you can hear the soaps while you cook.

b. Comb your hair. (You'll want to look good while you're cooking.)

c. Wash the dishes, clear the counters, and put everything away.

d. Put on a sexy outfit so your mate won't care that you can't cook.

2) What are the three reasons for washing your hands before you begin food preparation? (choose 3)

a. Because you will be touching things and then touching food.

b. You need clean hands to show you are conscientious.

c. Because dirty hands indicate a dirty house.

d. Because Mama said so.

e. Because you will eventually put your fingers in your mouth.

f. Your hands may come in contact with dead animals.

3) What is the best thing to do with your hair before cooking?

a. Wash it because it stinks.

b. Tie it up in a scarf or hairnet.

c. Cut it all off so you don't have to think about it.

d. None of the above.

4) What should you do to maintain a clean atmosphere throughout the cooking process?

a. Hire a dishwasher.

b. Put a bag in a bowl and throw your scraps in it.

c. Throw a tarp over the entire kitchen.

d. Put a bag in a bowl and then place it over your head.

5) Which two ingredients should you use to sanitize a wooden cutting board?

a. Vinegar and water

b. Oil and water

c. Alcohol and toothpaste

d. Rosemary and thyme

Sponge Cake Recipe

Ingredients :

5	eggs
1 cup	milk butter
250 ml	sifted cake flour
100 gr	sugar
1 tsp	baking powder

Oven temperature ~ 325 C
Baking time ~ 45 minutes
Pan type ~ 8 or 9 inch layer pans

Preheat oven, grease a small tube pan.
Beat egg yolks and sugar together until very light.
Melt milk butter and added to the ingredient.
Sift together flour and baking powder.
Add to batter. Beat egg whites until stiff. Fold into batter.
Pour batter into prepared pan.
Bake. Cool completely and invert onto cake platter.
Prepare whipped cream and strawberries.
To serve, slice cake in half and fill with half the whipped cream.
Top with remaining whipped cream and strawberries.

Organization

- Measurements
- Bakeware
- Heating Elements
- Cookware
- Tools

"All cooking is a matter of time.
In general, the more time the better."

—*John Erskine*

Measurements

To help you stay organized, make it a habit to measure all your ingredients in advance and place them in small glass custard cups.

Likely you've seen chefs on TV use these to show you exact amounts. You can even use ramekins if that's all you have. Preparing your amounts in advance is a great time-saver and prevents rushing around at the last minute and possibly ruining the recipe.

Read your recipe through at least once before you begin, and then pull out your little cups. Review how much of each small ingredient you will need. Custard cups are good for holding spices as well as herbs, cornstarch, baking powder or baking soda. You can use them to hold your diced garlic and shallots too.

It would be a good idea to invest in a few steel bowls of various sizes as well. These are good for measuring out sugar, flour, corn meal or Bisquick mix. And don't forget to have on hand a good set of measuring spoons and cups. Measuring cups come in two varieties: dry and liquid.

The dry cups come in plastic or aluminum and are for your dry ingredients (flour, sugar, cornmeal). Liquid cups are for wet ingredients such as water, milk, wine and broth. They are usually plastic or glass.

Both work equally well.

When you buy liquid measuring tools, look closely to see which measuring system is used. U.S. customary units are the standard in the states, which uses ounces, cups, pints, quarts and gallons. The United States has not yet adopted the International System of Units (the metric system) even though it is widely used in science and the military.

The best measuring utensils for liquids come with marks for both cups and ounces (oz.). Some come with marks in milliliters (ml), but if you are not comfortable calculating the conversion on the spot, it's best to go with the former. Measuring spoons are fairly straightforward. They come in 1/8, ¼, ½ and 1 teaspoon; ½ and 1 tablespoon. In most recipes these measures will be represented this way: the small letter *t* for teaspoon and the large letter *T* for tablespoon with the amount just below it or beside it, as in 1T or 2t. They are made to correspond with the ingredient amounts in your recipes.

Measuring spoons come in all materials, sizes, colors and shapes, including hearts or even daisies. They can be plastic, aluminum or glass. Some are white, others multi-colored. You can also get them in a combination of spoons and cups. But no matter the design, the measurements are always the same.

When using measuring spoons or cups, remember to put the amounts in your glass prep dishes for easy addition into your recipe.

Note: I will discuss cooking by sight in the **Success** section, but for now it is best that you measure everything until you have performed the recipe enough times to "eyeball" your ingredients.

Finally, it would also be a good idea to invest in a kitchen scale. This will ensure you use the correct measurements for recipes that provide weight instead of volume. See the **Appendix** for a conversion chart of common measurements.

Cookware

There are so many different kinds of what Mama used to call "pots 'n' pans." They come in different styles, weights, materials, and brands. In this section I will discuss these differences and what they mean for the types of food you plan to cook. First, let's review the basic materials with which pots and pans are made.

Cast Iron

It is said that in the 1700s an English Quaker named Abraham Darby was responsible for the casting process that brought us cast iron

Mama's Tip

Enamel-coated cast iron is also durable and goes easily from stove to oven, but not all brands are "oven-proof," which means they don't all withstand the same heat. Check the label to see temperature limits before using this cookware.

skillets and other pots and pans. Cast iron is a favorite among good cooks because it cooks evenly and consistently. Since it is heavy and sturdy, cast iron is made to last, and it does if you take care of it. The newer cast iron pots come already seasoned, but if you bought one of the traditional ones you must season it. To do this, pour a little cooking oil into the skillet, wipe it around the inside with a paper towel to ensure good coverage, and then bake it in the oven. The directions usually come with the new skillets. Once this curing takes place, the skillet will become darker and will be ready to serve you for years to come. Each time you wash the skillet, once it is clean and dry pour a few drops of oil into it and wipe it again with a paper towel. This will prevent rust.

Aluminum

Likely you have already experienced the versatility of aluminum. It's the material used in your canned goods, the tray for your dinner rolls, or the throwaway pans you use for baking lasagna. You may have seen cooks line the oven or BBQ rack with aluminum foil to catch drippings. Or maybe they used it to cover a turkey so it did not over brown.

Aluminum conducts heat, meaning it moves it away or spreads it around. There are several types of aluminum cookware; some are made from sheets while others are anodized. There are some health concerns regarding aluminum cookware, so do your research before you purchase.

Sheet aluminum is lighter and used for baking, such as with cookie sheets or cake pans. Cast aluminum is used for heavier pans and doesn't conduct heat as well. Anodized aluminum cookware is created through what's known as hard anodizing. It is the electrochemical processing of raw aluminum. The non-stick variety is becoming very popular among cooks because it is coated, preventing the acidic reaction that occurs with other aluminums when it comes in contact with foods such as tomato sauce. Anodized aluminum pots can be found under such brand names as Anolon and Calphalon. These brands can be expensive, so I suggest getting the off-season versions at a discount store like Marshall's or HomeGoods to save money.

Copper

If your only exposure to copper is the pipes in your bathroom, you'll find that it has many other uses, pots included. Copper is great for cooking because it heats up fast. You can get solid copper pots lined with tin to ward off sticking. But copper's upkeep takes more effort than some of the other materials mentioned here. It can turn green like the Statue of Liberty after years of use. To restore it, use a common copper or brass cleaner from the grocery store. Copper-bottom pots and pans are also available under the Revere Ware label. If you want solid copper cookware, as of this writing, a company called Hammer-smith in Brooklyn, New York, still makes it. But like some anodized brands, it's not cheap. You'll pay a few hundred bucks a pot, if not more.

Stainless Steel

This material has been in use for cooking since the early 1900s. Most cookware is made from stainless steel as a rule, because of its low price, good looks and ease of use (you can put these pots in the dishwasher). It is lighter than cast iron, but it does not cook as evenly unless it has a heat conducting assistant sandwiched in the middle, such as aluminum. This type of stainless steel cookware is known as tri-ply or three-ply. It is easy to clean and can last a long time, depending on the manufacturer. Unlike cast iron, copper, or aluminum, stainless steel is non-porous, which means it is resistant to harboring bacteria. But be aware that stainless steel is made with nickel, to which some people are allergic. Most nickel allergies stem from cheap jewelry that comes in contact with the skin, but if you or someone in your family has high nickel sensitivity, check the material of your chosen brand before you buy. The underside of the pot will tell you the amount of nickel it contains. If it says 18/8, it has 18 percent chromium and 8 percent nickel. If it says 18/10, it has 10 percent nickel. According to the Nickel Institute, these pots and pans do not pose a risk to those who are not highly nickel sensitive.

Non-stick (Teflon)

This material is actually a coating available on either stainless steel or aluminum cookware. A synthetic called polytetrafluoroethylene (PTFE) is bonded with aluminum, resulting in a non-stick surface. In 1954 Marc Gregoire of France developed the process that led to its use in cookware. The most popular non-stick product is best known under the brand name Teflon and the cookware label Tefal (pronounced and sometimes spelled T-Fal), which is a contraction of the two words Teflon and aluminum.

I like the convenience of a non-stick pan, but if not made well, over time they can get damaged; especially if you don't remember to always

use plastic or wooden utensils. The safety of the coatings have also come into question; however, the Teflon website (Teflon.com) has a list of myth busters regarding the safety of non-stick coatings. You should check it out. More expensive cookware makers, such as Staub, claim to use a tougher non-stick surface that resists scratching. Anodized non-stick pans are becoming very popular in the United States due to their ease of use and even cooking. As with any cookware, I would suggest you buy one piece and try it out before committing to an entire set.

Glass

Using glass on the stove is a definite no-no, but some forms of glass are great for oven use. Pyrex® is one example. It was introduced to cooks in 1915 by the Corning Company. In fact, the wife of a Corning Glass Works scientist came up with the idea. Another material—more sturdy than plain glass—was already in use for the company's railroad signal lanterns, and this woman wanted that material turned into a casserole dish! Ever since then cooks have relied on this convenient product. But be cautioned: Pyrex can shatter if taken from heat to cold too quickly. Allow time for hot items to cool in Pyrex before putting them in the refrigerator. I would never freeze Pyrex either. World Kitchen, which now manufactures Pyrex, has four recommendations for using its product:

1) Always place hot glass bakeware on a dry cloth potholder or towel. Never place hot glass bakeware on top of the stove, on a metal trivet, on a damp towel, or directly on a counter or sink.

2) Never put glass bakeware directly on a burner or under a broiler.

3) Always allow the oven to fully preheat before placing glass bakeware in the oven.

4) Always cover the bottom of the glass bakeware dish with liquid before cooking meat or vegetables.

Silicone

Since I am on the subject of baking, I'm mentioning this material because it is fast becoming a popular choice by good cooks. Its main advantage is ease of use. You can bend silicone, which makes removing baked goods a breeze. It also withstands high heat (up to 650 degrees) and it's light and easy to keep clean.

Types

Now that we know something about the heat conductivity of each material, let's review the basic types of pots and pans you will need to cook just about anything. For most good cooks, there are three essentials: the frying pan, the saucepan and the stockpot.

Frying pan

The frying pan (or skillet) is the mainstay of the American kitchen. Actually, that may be the case for kitchens worldwide. It is a flat pan, usually round but sometimes square. The standard sizes are 10 and 12 inch, though you can find them larger and smaller. It can be stainless steel, either heavy or light. It can be cast iron. It is also available in a few new materials introduced to the modern kitchen in the last few decades. So what type is best? Most good cooks will tell you that the cast iron skillet is best for frying, especially chicken and pork chops, or searing a steak. You can even bake cornbread in it!

As I mentioned earlier, non-anodized stainless steel is useful for lighter cooking, such as sautéing or simmering certain sauces. The anodized fryers can be used much the same way as cast iron.

You can use anodized or non-anodized frying pans to sweat onions and garlic because it is easier to move them around in the pan. They are also good for melting butter without changing its color, as cast iron tends to do.

I fry so much chicken in my cast iron skillet that it has a brown residue in it. But I like that residue so I intentionally don't clean all the

grease out of that pan; therefore, I can't use it for anything else. Besides that, the non-anodized pan is a lighter color so I can more easily see the onions turning translucent, but that's just me; you will develop your own preferences as you go. (I will discuss such terms such as "translucent" in more detail in the Success section.)

To make it easier to choose the proper fryer, here is a list of items I would cook / melt in a cast iron or anodized skillet compared to a non-anodized stainless steel one. As you get more familiar with pots and pans you will come to have your own favorites and personal preferences.

CAST IRON (anodized)	STAINLESS STEEL (non-anodized)
Fried chicken	White wine sauce
Fried pork chops	Sautéed vegetables (squash, or mushrooms)
Fried fish	Sautéed shrimp or scallops
Salmon croquettes	Butter (to melt)

Again, this list will vary slightly depending on the cook's preferences. You can use a saucepan for some of the items under the stainless steel skillet, like the wine sauce or the butter, but in my kitchen, saucepans are usually being used for other items, so the frying pan just comes in handy.

Saucepan

Saucepans usually come in 1-, 2- and 4-quart options. Some are larger, but these are the basic sizes. You will also see them advertised as sauteuse or saucier pans. The saucepan also comes in a variety of surfaces, and one is not really much better than the other. That is because most ingredients that go in the saucepan are liquid based and do not require any special treatment—you add the item, turn the heat on, put the lid on it and there you go. I also use saucepans for canned vegetables and beans, soup and instant gravy.

If I'm making frozen vegetables, I pour them into the saucepan (about half a 10 oz. bag fits nicely in a 2-quart pan) and then add a little water to prevent sticking. While they are cooking, I put the pan on low or medium with the lid on so the water will thaw out the vegetables. I check them every few minutes. That is the only time I worry about burning anything in a saucepan. Of course, if your saucepan is non-stick, this may not be an issue, as long as you keep an eye on it.

Be careful when lifting a saucepan. Some, as in the photo above, have rubber or plastic handles and can be grabbed with your bare hands. Others are made of the same material as the actual pan and tend to get very hot. It is always best to use a pot holder or mitt to pick up a saucepan to avoid burns.

Another practice I would recommend is keeping the handles pointed inward, meaning facing the wall of the stove. If you have small children, they will inevitably reach up to pull on the enticing handle of a saucepan. This, as you can imagine, could lead to disastrous results.

Stockpot

The stockpot is usually about 6 quarts, but some manufacturers are changing not only the size of these mainstays but also the name. Nowadays, it is referred to as a soup or chili pot. The original stock pot was called a Dutch oven and it was cast iron. It was used as a substitute for your real oven. I use both the original and the enamel-coated variety. I use my anodized stockpot for cooking soup and chili or boiling potatoes.

A true stockpot holds about 8 quarts. You can also cook the above items in this pot if you need to prepare larger amounts. I usually use this pot for boiling spaghetti. It can come with a built-in strainer to assist in disposing of the water once the spaghetti is cooked. It's a nice feature to prevent you from burning yourself with the hot water.

There are two more traditional stockpots, one is 10 quarts and the other is 16 quarts. The 16-quart pot is for large families that cook large volumes of chili or spaghetti. You will not likely need this big of a pot in your everyday cooking.

Wok

The wok is probably one of the oldest cooking tools known to man. Originating in China, it has become popular outside Asia for many reasons, not the least of which are its cooking speed and stiring technique.

Traditional woks are made of carbon steel, but some can be found in cast iron. Usually crafted with a rounded bottom, you will commonly see them sold with a rim to hold them upright. Newer woks, like the one in the photo, have flat bottoms. Cooking stir-fry style is very popular with the diet-conscious cook. The wok is shaped like a bowl so that the cook can get the most heat with the least amount of fuel. However, if you've ever had Chinese take-out, you've seen the high-flying flames around their woks. Keep in mind that they've been doing this for years. I would not recommend using such high flames at home. Woks are not just for stir-frying. You can also steam, braise or simmer using a few attachments. Unless it's non-stick the wok must also be seasoned. As you use your wok, don't be concerned when it starts to turn dark brown;

that's when the wok is at its best.

When cooking in the wok, the type of oil you use will determine whether you burn your food or cook it to perfection. For the best results, use oils with a high tolerance for heat, otherwise known as a high "smoke point." This includes peanut, corn and soybean oil. In addition, refined oil is better than unrefined because the smoke points are higher. You can find smoke point tables on the Internet. Never use butter or lard as an oil substitute in a wok!

When cooking in the wok, use constant quick strokes to ensure that the food does not stick and that it cooks evenly. It should be only a matter of minutes before the food is fully cooked. If you need to, go back to the take-out joint and watch how they do it. I will caution you that the technique they use of throwing the food in the air takes time to master; so if you don't want your meal to end up on the floor, skip that part of the lesson. Stirring will get the job done just as well.

If you are a die-hard wok enthusiast, you might want to check out the book *The Breath of a Wok* by Grace Young (Simon & Schuster). She goes into great detail regarding its origins and shares her childhood experiences growing up with an appreciation of 'wok hay.'

Bakeware

*W*e won't spend a lot of time on this because it is fairly straight-forward. The most-used bakeware in my kitchen are the cookie sheet, the muffin pan, the cake pan and the pie pan. Other baking tasks use various Pyrex pans, as I mentioned, as well as roasters. Let's briefly review some of this bakeware.

Cookie sheet

Cookie sheets come in regular aluminum, silicone and non-stick. If your cookie sheet is regular aluminum, always coat it with a little cooking oil spray before adding your cookies or other treats to it. To ensure your cookies do not burn, I recommend using an insulated cookie sheet. They bake more evenly than regular cookie sheets.

Muffin pan

The muffin pan typically comes in 6- and 12-cup sizes as well as minis, and can be regular aluminum or non-stick. This pan also comes in silicone for easy muffin removal. You can bake cupcakes in this pan as well as cornbread, gingerbread or homemade dinner rolls. If you are baking cupcakes, good cooks recommend you use paper liners made especially for this purpose. They prevent sticking, make cleanup a breeze and are fun for kids to pull off during the eating. You can get these liners in traditional white or other colors, as well as designs for special occasions. Look in the flour and sugar aisle of your grocery.

Cake pan

This pan comes in several shapes and sizes, as well as materials. The typical cake pan is aluminum and 9 inches around. You can use cake pans for single or multi-layer cakes as well as for heating up store-bought dinner rolls. Cake pans can be round, square or oblong. They come in aluminum, glass and silicone. When baking a cake, some recipes call for you to place parchment rounds inside to prevent sticking. This is just parchment paper you get from the grocery and cut into the shape of your pan. You can also use butter or baking spray to keep your cake from sticking.

One tip I recommend for removing a cake from the pan is to first allow it to completely cool, then take a butter knife and pressing against the side of the pan, and away from the cake, loosen it with one consistent motion. Then place your palm atop the middle of the cake and carefully turn it over. While holding the pan upside down in your palm, take that same butter knife and tap all around the bottom of the pan. This will loosen it. Gently lay the pan down on a plate, sliding your palm out from under the cake. Remove the pan.

Pie pan

Pie pans are much the same as cake pans in that they come in both aluminum and glass and they are usually about 9 inches around. I prefer PYREX (as opposed to Pyrex) pie pans because they are heavier and glass is just a nicer look for pie. Pies have a wonderful history too that I will take this time to share. Did you know that the first pies were made in the days of the Egyptians? Followed by the Greeks, then the Romans, a pie (spelled pye then) was usually more about the filling than the container. They did not use crust back then but rather reeds or other items to hold the filling; the outside was not meant for eating. Most early pies were made of meat and not fruit. Fruit pies did not come along until centuries later.

Roaster

Roasters are large, shallow pans that can hold a roast. But they can also be used for baking chicken, duck, fish or just about any other meat. I use the roaster for baking turkey, too. But in that case, always insert a roasting rack so the juices run out of the bird and into the pan. The rack makes it easy to remove the turkey and prevents it from soaking in its own juice. You can use that juice to make gravy.

Casserole dish (PYREX)

As shown in the glass photo, the casserole dish can be round or oval and come with a top or rectangular without a top. They can be used for macaroni and cheese, scalloped potatoes, or any other casserole-type dish. You will want to butter the dish before adding your ingredients to prevent sticking and to give the casserole some homemade flavor. Spread a thin layer of butter in the dish with your fingers. Be sure your hands are clean first! Then just press about a tablespoon of butter around to cover the bottom and sides of the dish.

Tools

When cooking any dish, there are a few basic utensils you will always need:

1. Spoons (wood, plastic, metal; slotted and flat)

2. Spatulas

3. Forks

These items are used mainly for stirring and should be paired with the proper cookware, as shown below:

COOKWARE	UTENSILS
Stainless steel	Wood, plastic, silicone
Non-stick	Wood, plastic, silicone
Cast iron	Wood, plastic, metal, silicone
Glass	Wood, plastic, metal, silicone

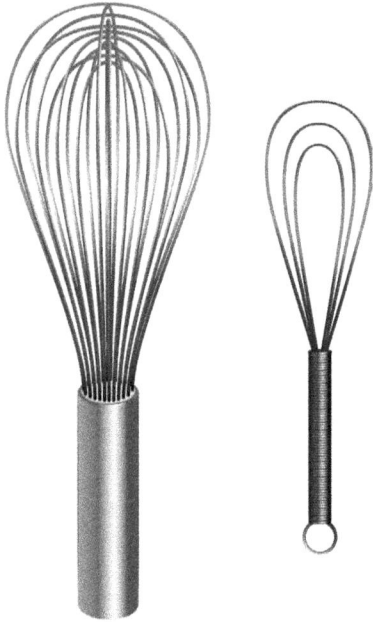

Wire whisks are a more practical choice than silicone. Make sure you get the kind with a solid handle as opposed to one with wire from top to bottom. Otherwise you will eventually see rust particles falling into your food as you mix.

Regarding silicone, keep in mind that it is soft and flexible, so if you need a firm spoon for a task, either do not use silicone or choose a silicone-coated metal utensil. Silicone utensils may not withstand the high temperatures that silicone cookware does, so be careful where you use them. Ensure that you choose food-grade silicone that is approved by the FDA.

Ancillary Tools

I'm including a list of other utensils not considered "basic" but still commonly used in a good cook's kitchen. You may want to acquire these for your future cooking needs:

- Tongs - for grabbing things
- Pastry brush - for basting or applying
- Grater - for scraping the skin from lemons (known as zest)

As you try more and more recipes you will begin to purchase other utensils. Just be sure you are going to use them at least a few times a month or they may not be worth the money.

Work horses

What separates the cooks from the kooks in the kitchen? The answer is machines. I'm talking about those essential items you will need to take your meals from just fair to fantabulous!

The Standing Mixer

One of my favorite tools is the standing mixer. It's the mixer that comes with a big steel bowl and looks industrial. At this writing, KitchenAid makes one of the more popular brands, the Artisan.

The first KitchenAid mixer for home use was built in 1919 in my neck of woods, Springfield, Ohio. The H-5 mixer was manufactured at the Troy Metal Products plant under the Hobart Corporation. As the story goes, a company executive's wife used the mixer and called it the

"best kitchen aid" a woman could have and that's how it got the name KitchenAid. The factory was later moved to Greenville, Ohio, where—as of this writing—the mixers are still made.

This mixer usually comes with—or you can buy—a variety of attachments to make homemade pasta, grind meat, or even prepare soft ice cream. It is awesome for making breads and cookies too. Aside from its versatility, this tool makes cooking a joy. How? It does much of the work for you and that's what you want in the kitchen: reliable help.

Before you go to a big department store to purchase this tool, check the outlets and strip malls. I saw one the other day for $179. That may seem high, but that first mixer in 1919 cost even more! Believe me, this mixer NEVER goes on sale for less than $249. And if you get it at that price, it's still a good deal. Go online to price them for yourself. They typically run about $350 retail. You should also look out for coupon sales at Bloomingdale's. Yes, believe it or not, that high-end retailer has a coupon sale that comes along once in a while and brings the price of this mixer down to $199. Don't be afraid to ask the clerk about it. He or she may be able to get you the discount on sight.

Once you get your hands on this mixer, the first thing you'll notice is its weight. Take my advice: anything heavy is good (like the cast iron skillet). That is another reason why it is so expensive—it lasts. I've had my mixer going on 11 years now, and it works just as well as it did the first time.

If you make cookies or cakes, this mixer is the best way to ensure your ingredients are blended together properly because the mixing motion is consistent, unlike doing it by hand. For recipes that call for alternating ingredients (See the **How-tos** section), use this mixer for best results. Cookie dough is especially error-free too. I make a really easy oatmeal and raisin recipe I got off the back of the Quaker Oats box, and it's a cinch to throw together at the last minute. I put all the ingredients in at the same time and then crank up the mixer. It is that simple. In no time, the dough is ready to be spooned onto the cookie sheet.

You will learn as you cook that time is either your friend or your enemy. Make the best use of it you can, and you will enjoy cooking even more. When I come home after working all day, the last thing I want to do is more work. But if I can acquire tools that shorten my time over the stove, then that is, for me, a beautiful thing.

The Food Processor

My second favorite tool is the food processor. Some people refer to it as a Cuisinart because it was so-named by its inventor, who capitalized on a French design seen a few years earlier. In 1973 both the Cuisinart food processor and the company of the same name came into existence.

The food processor not only allows you to mix, but its sharp, double-edged blades can also transform just about any solid food into liquid. You can use it for all your slicing and chopping needs too. I use it to quickly dice onions and peppers and to create soups from vegetable mixtures. Most food processors come with a couple of attachments to julienne potatoes or carrots, and it can slice French fries as well.

This tool can be a bit tricky to use. I got mine as a wedding gift and never used it because I thought it was broken. No matter what I did, the darn thing would not turn on. After it sat in the closet for about two years, I decided to pull it out and try it again. This time I called the manufacturer, and they walked me through the process. Turns out I was trying to lock the container onto the base from the wrong side. I also had to reset the thing to get the motor to run again. After I overcame these two hurdles, I was off and running. I've been using it consistently ever since. My advice: always read the instructions before

using any kitchen contraption.

Even if you have never used either of the above tools, this next one is sure to be on your shelf or kitchen counter.

The Blender

Everyone has found a use for the blender, especially since so many people are trying to be health conscious.

This tool was invented in 1922 by Stephen Poplawski and was refined over the years by many, including names you may know, such as Waring and Hamilton-Beach.

Most people use the blender to make drinks, like smoothies. I know more than a few people who use it to mix alcoholic drinks, but those uses are only the tip of the blender iceberg.

Some cooks use it to make vinaigrette dressing (herbed oil and vinegar) or sauces that accompany a meat dish. Again, read the instructions that come with your tools; sometimes they will provide free recipes that can give you some creative ideas for your own cooking projects.

If you plan to use your blender for a lot of cooking projects, you might consider getting one just for that purpose. I have two: one for mixing drinks and another for cooking. I would also suggest you get a blender that handles ice well. Continually crushing ice in a conventional blender can cause the blades to dull. Look for blender brands that specifically say they are good for crushing ice.

Heating Elements

No discussion of equipment would be complete without talking heat: your stove, oven, microwave or any other plug-in you choose to get your meal to the table.

Ovens

Ovens, for example, can be especially tricky. It is important to remember that no two are alike. So you should be familiar with *how* your oven cooks food.

For instance, a recipe may tell you to preheat the oven to 350 degrees and cook for 45 minutes. But after 45 minutes your food is still not done, or worse, it's over-cooked. This intricacy is something recipe books cannot tell you for your particular oven. Therefore, you should always test a recipe before preparing it for others. If you do this, you can work out all the "kinks" and be confident once you are ready to present your new dish to the general public.

Mama's Tip

Before you turn on the oven, always check for burnt food that dropped from the pan during your last meal. If you get rid of these crispy critters beforehand, you won't end up with a smoky kitchen and an oven too hot to clean right away.

I have a Jenn-Air double oven, which replaced the builder's-grade oven that was installed when I bought the house. The Jenn-Air oven does not take as long to cook some foods as the builder's oven did. I found that out when I tried to bake my famous carrot cake. I was not about to let the carrot cake—which I had been making for more than 20 years—overcook in the Jenn-Air, so I watched it carefully. I discovered the cake needed about 10 minutes less cooking time in this new oven than in the builder's grade. This was good news for me, as I can now get my cake to the table faster.

Oven cleaning should be done at least once a month. Use a cleaner like Easy Off No-Fume so you don't hack your way through the process. A clean oven cooks better and faster.

Stoves

There has probably been debate over stove preferences since it was invented. Some cooks prefer gas, while others prefer electric. Some want burner grates while others like a smooth surface. I prefer gas and grates. Five or even six burners are ideal, though most stoves come with just the basic four.

When I was a child, my father was into gadgets. He bought my mother a trash incinerator and a cooktop stove. The stove had lines instead of burner grates, and they turned red when the stove was on. That was amazing to see in 1969. The cooktop was manufactured by Corning and, of course, you could only use CorningWare on it. Unfortunately, it didn't get very hot, and you could not brown anything in those glass pots. Several cooks who use them say today's glass stovetops are good performers. But the fact is none of the top chefs use them. I say everyone to his own taste.

The tools of cooking should be practical enough to support the task at hand; if it also looks cool that's just a bonus.

The stove in my current home is a stainless-steel cooktop, and it is not the easiest thing to keep clean or scratch free. The best product for this is a non-abrasive cleaner designed specifically for stainless steel. After it cools, wash the stove off with a damp Handi Wipe®. Most stoves these days can be disassembled for complete cleaning under the grates and sometimes the burner apparatus too.

To clean the grates better, I soak them in hot water using a degreasing dish liquid such as Dawn or Greased Lightning. That helps tremendously with removing any dried-on gunk.

Microwaves

These days just about everyone either owns or has used a microwave oven. It is a very practical machine, but I use it for only two things: heating up and defrosting. (Note: Be careful not to heat food for too long lest it become rubbery and inedible.)

Convection microwaves seem to be all the rage now. They can bake, broil and roast. They beat a traditional microwave because they cook, not just reheat, and they do so in less time than an oven. How? By circulating the heated air around the food and using the moisture from the food to assist. An added plus is that convection ovens can brown food.

Here's the downside: Convection ovens are not cheap unless you find one at a Sears Outlet or similar store. And the counter space they take up may make them impractical for some kitchens, unless you buy one that is installed above the stove. They can be a good investment for someone with a very small kitchen or for a cook who needs an extra oven.

The convection microwave I used to own blew up! Suffice it to say I am now using my regular oven exclusively.

Temperatures

On a stove, the temperature knobs are typically labeled as High, Medium, and Low. But what does this really mean? In general terms, High means boiling, Medium means a low boil, and Low means not yet boiling. But to be specific, most burner heat is measured in BTUs (British Thermal Units).

One BTU is the amount of heat needed to heat one pound of water by one degree Fahrenheit. That may not mean anything to you and it doesn't to most people. What's important to know is that each burner on your stove has a BTU level that is designed for a specific purpose. For instance, your higher BTUs are on the larger burners, for boiling.

Usually recipes will tell you to lower the temperature (or flame) so that the food can continue to cook once it is at the boiling point. That is what the Medium or intermediate flame level is for. Food will not cook any faster when a higher flame setting is used than is necessary to maintain a gentle boil. Water boils at the same temperature whether boiling gently or vigorously. Use Low to simmer foods, keep them warm or melt things like chocolate or butter. These are your lowest-BTU burners.

Just as with your oven, when it comes to temperature, success depends on your particular stove. Common sense is the key when frying food: if the heat is too high, it's going to burn, too low and it won't cook all the way through, unless you are simmering for an extended period of time. This is going to be a trial-and-error exercise, and no one can really tell you the results unless they have cooked in your kitchen. Be sure to use just as much oil as is necessary to fry your food. Too much oil will splatter and you could get burned. Oil should never rise up the sides of your meat (unless you are frying chicken), but should instead be just below. You should always heat the oil in the pan before adding the meat. If you attempt to cook in a cold pan of oil, the meat will soak up the oil and ruin your meal. When I was a kid, Mama used to throw a few drops of water in the oil to test if it was heated. But that is not necessary with today's pans. When the oil is hot, you should notice hundreds of tiny bubbles in the bottom. This is a good indication that the oil is ready to accept your meat or fish.

In the oven, one thing remains the same no matter what kind you have: all ovens lose heat each time you open to check on your food. Re-

Mama's Tip

No matter what method you use to cook your meat, it needs to rest before cutting and eating because it is still cooking inside. Take it off the stove or out of the oven, put foil over it, and then let your meat rest for at least 15 minutes.

sist

doing this! It will only increase the cooking time and it could ruin your dish because of the lost heat. Look through the oven window instead.

 When baking there is no standard temperature; the heat will depend on the item you bake. Always remember to preheat your oven before baking; that simply means you wait until the oven reaches your desired temperature before adding the food.

Most things cook well at 350 degrees, but certain desserts must be cooked at 325. Other recipes will require the heat to be as high as 400, and if a quick browning is required, 500 may be recommended. Again, know your heating elements and the intensity your pots can handle.

Timing is also something to consider in a discussion of temperatures. Use a timer. I've often put something in the oven or on the stove and walked away, forgetting to come back and check it on time. A timer is a good reminder to stop whatever you are doing and check on your food. Just be sure you set the time as soon as you start the dish and promptly check when the timer goes off.

Organization Quiz

Now that we have discussed Organization at length, let's take a quick quiz:

1) Which cookware should you avoid if you or a dinner guest is highly sensitive to nickel?

a. Cast iron

b. Copper

c. Aluminum

d. Stainless steel

2) According to the makers of Pyrex, what should you never do with this cookware when it is hot?

a. Place it on the stove

b. Place it on a metal rivet

c. Place it on a wet towel

d. Place it on the sink

e. All of the above

3) **What kind of oil should NOT be used in a wok?**

a. Crisco
e. Unrefined

b. Butter
f. a, b, c

c. Olive
g. a, b, c and e

d. Peanut
h. All of the above

4) **How can you tell when oil is hot enough for cooking?**

a. By touching it

b. By noticing the tiny rolling bubbles at the bottom

c. By throwing water in it

d. None of the above

5) **What are the two best utensils to use in any cookware?**

a. Metal and silicone

b. Metal and wood

c. Silicone and wood

d. Silicone and plastic

Technique

"Non-cooks think it's silly to invest
two hours' work in two minutes' enjoyment;
but if cooking is evanescent, so is the ballet."

— *Julia Child*

Main Dish

*N*ow we come to the star of the show: your main dish. This is usually meat, chicken (poultry) or fish, but for those who are health conscious, it could be a vegetable or even tofu.

Main dishes must be the best part of your meal. They should never be overshadowed by a side dish. The only exception can be dessert, for obvious reasons.

There are countless ways you can prepare and serve main dishes, so let's focus on buying and choosing the right ones.

Vegetables and Tofu

When you go to the grocery to buy vegetables, it is a common and wise practice to ensure an item is fresh by 1) feeling it, and that it is ripe by 2) observing it. For instance, most vegetables are not meant to be eaten green. The exceptions are those that are supposed to be green, such as peas or broccoli. Tomatoes can be eaten red or green, depending on your taste.

When feeling certain vegetables, they should be firm not soft. Butternut squash, for example, should also appear matte and not shiny. On the other hand, a shiny eggplant with deep purple skin is an excellent choice. If you are unsure about how your main dish vegetable should look and feel, the produce manager at your grocery will be happy to help you make the best choice.

Tofu is used as a main dish for many vegetarians because it is so versatile. It has no flavor of its own but takes on the flavors you add to it. How neat is that? But choosing tofu can be tricky because its consistency depends on the recipe you are using. Some tofu is soft while others are firm. I am not a tofu expert, but my vegetarian friends suggest you always buy it at a health food store or Asian market for best results. The cake should be white and the water in the package should be clear. Drain it. Put a paper towel on a plate and then place the tofu on top. Put another paper towel over the tofu and press down. Use something weighty like an old book or can of veggies to hold it down for about 20 minutes. Whatever you use it is bound to get wet so if you use books, choose wisely.

Change the water in your tofu as soon as you get it home to keep it from spoiling too fast. Always check the expiration date on the package as well.

The Nasoya website, which makes the tofu I sometimes use, has this advice for choosing tofu:

TOFU TYPE	USE
Extra firm	Stir frying
Firm	Baking
Cubed	Salads
Soft	Dips and soups
Silken	Smoothies

For more specific instructions on how to prepare these types of tofu, visit **http://www.nasoya.com/how-to/what-to-do-with-tofu.html**.

Fish

Most people believe that if fish smells fishy, there is probably something fishy going on inside. But that is not the case for all fish, such as sardines. The truth is that fish is going to smell…well, like fish. The smell is normal and is caused by organic compounds called amines. The best way to get rid of this odor in fish is to counteract it with something else. You can use lemon juice, vinegar or even baking soda to accomplish this because their acidic nature counteracts the alkaline effects of the amines and thus eliminates the odor. Most people squeeze lemon juice on fish before eating it at a restaurant and just before cooking. Now you know why. In contrast, fish with a very strong odor is likely spoiled.

When buying fish at the grocery, ask yourself these questions:

Do I want the skin on or off? Some skin-on fish come with scales that can get under your skin or stuck in your mouth. When I was young, living in San Francisco, I bought ocean perch, which came with the scales on it. Not being a very experienced cook in those days, I tried to remove them myself. Bad move. Unfortunately, they got under my skin and were very irritating. If you want to keep the skin on your fish, ask the butcher to remove the scales for you.

Do I want a whole fish or a filleted fish? You can get both at the grocery or farmer's market, either already scaled and gutted with the head and fins still on, or as-is, meaning you must do the scaling and gutting at home.

I suggest you buy a whole fish already "dressed" so you do not have to perform these additional steps.

Filleted fish can be skin-on or off, but with the head and tail removed as well as any bones. Filleted fish is the most common treatment you will see in grocery stores. It is usually kept on ice to preserve its freshness.

Meat & Poultry

Beef, pork and poultry are usually sold in packag-

Mama's Tip

Never cook anything else in the same oil you used to cook fish. The item will smell and taste like fish.

ing at the grocery, but you can also find it displayed the same as fresh fish, under a glass case. You can find better cuts of meat at specialty stores such as Whole Foods and Trader Joe's, or at the butcher shop. They will usually offer a wider variety as well.

When choosing beef, the color is the first indicator of freshness. Don't buy meat that has a brownish-red color. The fat surrounding the meat will also be an off red, and the packaging may contain blood run off. Most beef that is about to go bad is sold on special for quick sale. If you buy beef like this, read the label indicating how soon it must be cooked. If you do not plan to cook it by that date, don't buy it. You could freeze it, but I wouldn't.

Pork is not truly red like beef, but rather a paler, pinkish hue. If it looks brown, it should be avoided. Pork is particularly susceptible to trichinosis, a larvae infection that can cause diarrhea and abdominal pain in humans. According to the Centers for Disease Control and Prevention, most pigs in the United States are raised in confined pens and feed is controlled, which has almost eliminated the disease here. But hogs raised outdoors are still likely to get infected, such as pork that is imported from other countries.

To avoid this infection, pork must be well cooked and never eaten raw. Always follow the safe handling instruction label on the package, which is required by the USDA. And just like with our germy chicken from chapter one, I suggest you wear plastic gloves when handling any raw meat; you should wash your hands before touching anything else.

When deciding on a chicken, whether whole or in pieces, pay attention to the labels. Some chickens are for frying while others are for baking. Whole frying chickens are of smaller weight; usually less than four pounds. A whole chicken good for baking is called a roaster. It is generally larger than a fryer and contains more fat. However, there is no hard and fast rule that says you cannot use these birds interchangeably, just know the differences are flavor and texture: the fryer is more tender, while the roaster will be more flavorful.

You may not be able to tell by looking at it, but if a chicken is spoiled, the bad odor definitely gives it away. The skin will also have a slimy texture it.

Storing Meat

*A*fter visiting the grocery store you will likely freeze most of the meat you buy. The best method is using freezer bags. However, the meat you intend to cook that day should go in the refrigerator. If you keep it in its original packaging, place a plate under it in case the juice from the packaging seeps out. Or you can remove the packaging and transfer it to a plastic container with a tight lid. Food that is in the refrigerator like this will not stay fresh long, so make sure you intend to use it in less than three days.

The same goes for food that has been cooked and refrigerated. If your family doesn't eat leftovers, this can become a problem and a lot of food will be wasted. The estimated amount of food waste that takes place in the United States each year in tons is, as of this writing, in the double-digit millions. That alone should be incentive enough for you to think twice before either buying too much food or cooking more than your family will eat.

To freeze the meat you buy, follow these tips for best results:

1. Get out your freezer bags, aluminum foil, or heavy plastic wrap.

   a. If you use freezer bags, write the day's date in the space provided with a magic marker.

b. If you use foil or wrap, tear off as much as you think you will need. Err on the side of more rather than less.

2. Put on your plastic gloves.

3. Remove the original meat packaging and discard; do not set it down on the counter.

4. If there are no dishes in the sink, rinse the meat and pat it dry with a towel.

5. Place the meat or fish in one of the preservation items you want to use.

6. Wrap it tight and make sure there are no open spaces.

7. Put it in the freezer.

Be sure not to leave meats or fish in the freezer too long or they will suffer from freezer burn. You can tell it from its extra-icy, crystallized appearance and dry, beige-looking color. Frozen food that is not burnt just looks natural, only solid.

Types of Meat

Some people rely on the grade of meat to determine its quality. Grading is done by the US Department of Agriculture (USDA) but the meat producer actually requests and pays for it.

Beef is graded one of two ways: by its quality or by its yield, meaning the amount of usable meat on the animal. Beef quality grades are prime, choice and select. Prime cuts are reserved for restaurants in most cases. You may not even see a grade on the meat you buy at the store, because some meats are sold under the store brand name, but if you run across any graded beef here is what you can expect:

GRADE	WHAT IT MEANS
Prime	Lots of fat (marbling); very juicy and tender. Roasts and steak cuts are the best.
Choice	Less marbling but still very tender and flavorful. Loin and rib cuts are best.
Select	Leaner and less flavorful. Loin, rib and sirloin cuts are the best.

Poultry is graded with the letters A, B or C. The **Grade A** shield is for whole birds and, according to the USDA, is typically the only grade you will find in retail stores. This grade means the chicken is free of defects, bruises, discolorations and feathers. **Grades B or C** are reserved for cut-up chickens, but be aware that your chicken's packaging may not display any grade. And trust me, the more you cook chicken, you *will* find a few feathers here and there. Just cut them off and keep moving.

Lamb is also regulated by the USDA. It is delicious with oil and hot peppers, with the fat on or off, and as a rack or chops. But a word of caution: after cooking lamb, never leave it out overnight. The smell will permeate your house. By the way, pork is inspected but not graded by the USDA.

Cooking Methods

There are so many varieties of beef, pork and poultry that they could not all possibly be covered in this book. So the next best thing is to tell you what is typically done with the most common types and your recipe books can take it from there. You may want to get a highlighter for this section so you can quickly refer back to it later:

Ground meat. Ground beef is usually used to make hamburgers, and it is the main ingredient in chili and spaghetti. Ground beef substitutes such as turkey or chicken can also be used. Ground pork is never used this way. It is too fatty. Use ground pork along with ground beef in meatloaf, or just fry it as a breakfast patty. The exception to this rule for spaghetti is Italian sausage, Andouille, chorizo or smoked sausage. All of these can be ground, made into meatballs, or sliced for a unique spaghetti sauce.

Steaks. A good steak is typically grilled or broiled, but some people fry them. Frying will deplete the flavor of steak and dry it out, so I do not recommend it. The only exception is cube steak or flank steak. Of course, you can always sear a steak on the stove and then bake it, but why do that to a wonderful piece of beef? Grilling is one of the best ways to bring out the rich flavor of steak.

Roasts. Roasts come in a few varieties. There's rib roast, rump roast and chuck roast, just to name a few. Ribs and rumps are baked and so is just about any other roast. Chuck roast is very good in a slow cooker and takes minimal effort to prepare.

Here is an easy recipe for chuck: cut some onions into fourths and then add them and some baby carrots to the slow cooker. Season your chuck roast with salt and pepper and then you can sear it in a fryer to brown it. Next, place the roast into the slow cooker. Sprinkle a packet of Lipton's Onion Soup mix on top of the roast. Pour in about a half-cup of beef broth, put the lid on the slow cooker and leave it to cook on low for four hours. The results will amaze you. This meal is also called pot roast.

Pork chops. Chops can be baked, grilled, broiled or fried depending on your taste. If you must fry them, just brown them and add a little water or broth to them. Lower the heat and put the lid on the fryer to finish cooking; this will maintain their tenderness. Remove the lid for the last few minutes to eliminate some of the moisture. If you desire, you can make gravy with the resulting juices .

Thick pork chops are best cooked in the oven so they can get good and done. But chops of about a half-inch thick are fine on the stove as long as you do not cook them over too much heat and dry them out. One way to do this is to sear then simmer. First, while wearing latex gloves, pour a little vegetable oil on each chop. Rub it all over the chop with your hands. The oil will make the seasoning stick and eliminate the need for more oil in the pan, especially if you sear them in a non-stick or anodized fryer. If using cast iron, you may want to use a little more oil, but not much because you don't want the pan to be oily. Heat the oil on medium high while you are seasoning the meat.

You can use salt, pepper, a little cayenne and some garlic powder. But get creative and try some new seasonings or herbs you think might go well with pork. Once they are browned on both sides, remove them to a plate. Add minced garlic and shallots to the pan and stir them just enough to get them soft. Now add a half-cup of broth or water. Return the chops to the pan and cook on low with a lid on until all the pink is gone.

Chicken drumsticks and wings. These can be cooked in the fryer, on the grill or in the oven. They are delicious regardless of the cooking method. I suggest keeping them in a bowl of ice water until just before you are ready to flour and fry them. By the way, I would not recommend frying legs that have the thigh still connected. You will see why in the next entry.

Chicken thighs and breasts. Because thighs and breasts are larger and contain more meat, they are best cooked in the oven. Baking helps them to cook more thoroughly. If you try to fry these pieces alongside wings or drumsticks, you will be disappointed because they will not cook as fast. Fry the thighs separately or only a few at a time. Unless they are boneless, thighs should be boiled or baked before grilling so they cook inside. Many a bird has been ruined on the grill, being cooked outside but not in.

Breasts, especially, are not favorites of Southern fried chicken enthusiasts. On the contrary, they love wings! As a novice cook, steer clear of the breasts. By the way, breasts do not make for good grilling either. Stick with wings and legs if possible. These do not have to be cooked in advance.

Whole chickens. Whole chickens (roasters) are baked in the oven, but you can cut them in half and brown them on the stove in a Dutch oven, and then transfer them to the regular oven to finish cooking. To enhance the tenderness of this chicken before cooking, soak it in a water and salt solution for about an hour, and then pat dry and season. This will keep the meat moist and tender. Season with sage, salt, and pepper inside and out, using gloves.

Fish fillets. Fillets are best fried but can be baked and broiled too. To fry fish, you coat it with corn meal or flour. I've even used crumbled Ritz crackers. I just take a plastic grocery bag, put in about a half-cup each of flour and cornmeal, add salt and pepper, garlic and onion powder, and paprika for color.

Then I throw my fish pieces in and shake up the bag. Once they are coated, I shake off the excess and set them in the hot oil on medium-high until they are crispy on the edges. Then I turn them over to repeat on the other side. Yummy!

Mama's Tip

Do not reuse flour once raw meat has been mixed in it. Use the bag once then throw it away. Even if your flour is in a plate or bowl, do not attempt to store it and reuse it!

Some cooks use an egg wash or milk after dipping them in flour and then they dip again in cornmeal. You can experiment and come up with your own style.

You can bake fish or broil it on high, but just for a short time. Whatever you are doing, follow the recipe or package directions and make a test batch before going all in.

Baking fish is easy and healthier than frying. Preheat your oven to 350 degrees. Lightly spray the fillets on both sides with cooking oil spray and then season them as you would to fry them, but skip the flour and cornmeal. Place your fillets in a shallow Pyrex pan. The fish will cook in about 20 minutes. You can test if it's done with a fork. If it flakes, it's done.

For a crusty baked fish, used crushed Ritz crackers mixed with melted butter. Sprinkle the mixture over the fillets and bake. This method adds more calories, but it does taste good. If you want to get fancy, you can bake the fish by steaming it while wrapped in aluminum foil. Lay the foil in the bottom of the dish, allowing enough to hang over the sides so you can wrap up the fish. You will need some sort of marinade or white wine mixture (look for marinades on the Internet) to help the steaming process. A lemon pepper marinade is always nice. Once you add the marinade, wrap the fish and bake at 400 degrees for about 20 minutes, depending on the type of fish. You need the higher heat because the fish is wrapped and foil conducts heat. Set your timer and check it. Be sure to use your potholders!

Side Dishes

What would a main dish be without sides? That second and third item on a perfectly arranged dinner plate is just as important, especially when you consider these are packed with vitamins and nutrients to compliment a protein-filled main dish.

Preparing sides begins with choosing the right combinations. For instance, your sides should complement the main dish in both color and texture. If you are cooking red meat, you might choose broccoli and a baked potato. Or you could choose yellow squash and sweet potatoes. But you do not have to have a starch and vegetable with the meal. You could choose to prepare two vegetables. Like cabbage and carrots, a combination used often with a Jamaican main dish of goat or chicken. These dishes usually include plantain, which is actually a fruit.

The key to selecting sides is to

Mama's Tip

When creating a large meal such as a turkey dinner, lots of side dishes are expected. In order not to become overwhelmed trying to prepare it all in one day, plan what you can prepare in advance. Macaroni and cheese, cakes, and homemade cranberry sauce can all be done the day before.

get color on the plate, which translates into providing the right mix of essentials for your consumers' health. How you prepare the sides determines how much nutrition they receive. The secret is to cook them just enough, not overdone or underdone.

Steaming is a great way to keep the nutrients intact. You can either invest in a steamer or you can create one. Add about a quart of water to a 2- or 3-quart saucepan, then put a colander on top that fits inside the pan and rests on the rim without falling in. Bring the water to a rolling boil and add broccoli, cauliflower or asparagus to the colander. Put a lid on the pot and allow it to steam the veggies for about 10 minutes. Be careful when removing the lid. Your vegetables should be shiny and still firm but not hard. Stick in a fork to test doneness. The fork should go in easily.

Salad is also a good side to offer with a main dish because it provides a variety of nutrients. Most people who don't know how to cook do know how to throw a salad together; if you don't, just visit your local buffet and see what's on the menu. It will give you some ideas for creating your own concoctions. The rule of thumb for salads is the same as for all sides: combining colors and textures. If you keep this in mind, you can't go wrong.

In the **Success** section under Basic How-tos, you will find a few techniques for preparing side dishes such as mashed potatoes, rice, cabbage and squash.

Seasoning

Nothing brings out the flavor of food like herbs. Fresh ones are the best, but the dried variety are good too. I like to buy herbs at the farmer's market or grow them myself. Growing herbs is easy and something to consider in light of how expensive fresh herbs can be. They also spoil rather quickly, which is another reason to grow them.

Dried herbs come in plastic containers at the farmer's market and are inexpensive. I pay as little as 35 cents per ounce, depending on the type of herb. Fresh herbs vary in price at the market, but are usually much less than at the grocery. You can find both fresh and dried herbs there. The dried ones will be in bottles. You may be alarmed when you see the price of bottled herbs, but you are paying mostly for that fancy container.

If you grow your own, it's easy to dry them yourself. To do this, tie the ends with a string and hang them upside down in a dry place for about two weeks. When dry, crush the leaves under a rolling pin or with a mortar and pestle and store them in an airtight plastic bag.

There are no hard and fast rules about which herbs to use for which dishes, but there are a few generally accepted practices. For instance, almost all Italian food is going to contain one or more of these herbs: thyme, basil, bay leaves and oregano. If you are cooking a Mexican dish, cilantro is likely going to be part of the recipe. There are also certain herbs that go naturally with certain meats, such as sage and poultry, or rosemary and lamb.

Spices

You will likely use spices even more than you use herbs. From your basic salt to the expensive saffron threads, spices do just that—they spice up just about anything you cook. The secret to great tasting food is to know which spice will bring out the essence of a particular meat, fish or vegetable. This takes time and practice, but can be easily mastered. Experimenting is the best way to go. Take the time to visit the local market and pick one out. Smell its aroma and imagine what it might complement. Then take it home and try it out. It's that simple.

I use certain spices every day, such as cinnamon and nutmeg for baking, turmeric and paprika in chicken dishes, and good old salt and pepper for just about everything.

Some spices come in the form of seeds, such as cumin or coriander. You can bring out the locked in flavor of these spices by crushing them with a mortar and pestle. This useful tool comes in many materials, but the best is marble because it is not porous and will not harbor smells or bacteria. You simply add the seeds into the mortar bowl, crush them with the pestle stick, and then add to your favorite recipe.

For an exhaustive list of herbs, spices and their uses, I recommend Jill Norman's book *Herbs & Spices: The Cook's Reference* (DK Publishing). In the meantime, here are some blends you can use right now:

Dried Herb Seasoning (for fish, chicken)

- 1T thyme

- 1T oregano

- 2t sage

- 1t rosemary

- 1t marjoram

- 1t basil

- 1t parsley flakes

Five Spice Powder (for fish, pork)

- 2t anise seeds, crushed

- 2t ground pepper

- 2t fennel seeds, crushed

- 2t ground cloves

- 2t ground cinnamon

- 1.5t ground ginger

- ½t ground allspice

Old Bay (a.k.a. Chesapeake Bay) Seasoning (for seafood, chicken)

- 1T ground bay leaves

- 2.5t celery salt

- 1.5t dry mustard

- 1.5t black pepper

- ¾t ground nutmeg

- ½t ground cloves

- ½t ground ginger

- ½t paprika

- ½t red pepper flakes

- ¼t mace

- ¼t cardamom

Cooking Liquids

It's important to mention the cooking liquids available to help flavor your dishes as well. Vinegar, liquid smoke, and chicken broth are just a few of the staples in my cooking repertoire. On the following page is a basic list and their uses.

Chicken broth

I use this as a base for many of my white sauces, such as white clam sauce. I also use it to flavor collards when I don't want to use fatback or other pork flavoring. Chicken broth is a good substitute for water when you want to add flavor to frozen vegetables. I use it when I need a little liquid at the bottom of a baked chicken dish, or when I am brining my turkey. I keep 3 or 4 boxes in the pantry because I always need it for something.

Hot sauce

This is not to be confused with hot pepper sauce, which has a completely different flavor. Hot sauce is red; hot pepper sauce is clear and usually contains the actual peppers in the bottle. Uses for hot sauce include chili, spaghetti and BBQ sauces you make from scratch. It can be added to give anything a little kick, but don't add too much or you won't be able to eat it. Hot pepper sauce is much hotter than regular hot sauce and is called for specifically in certain recipes.

Liquid smoke

This is one of my favorite flavor enhancers. It makes a variety of foods taste as if they were cooked on the grill. I use it in baked beans, green beans, collards, and in my homemade BBQ sauce. You can find it in the condiment aisle at your grocery store.

Soy sauce

This dark liquid is a classic in Asian cooking and can be very salty;

it also comes in a low-sodium variety that is just as tasty as the original. Soy sauce can also be used as an ingredient in homemade BBQ sauce and enhances the flavor of just about any rice dish, if used sparingly.

Worcestershire sauce

This sauce is typically associated with steak, but it makes any beef dish taste much better. It is also good on pork and lamb. It is a traditional flavor in beef stroganoff.

Vinegar

Vinegar—whether white, red, or apple cider—is something no Southern cook can do without. Vinegar is a mainstay for cooking greens and green beans. It is also a standard ingredient for BBQ sauce, especially in the Southeastern states. But again, caution is advised because too much is too much. Balsamic and tarragon vinegar are ideal for vinaigrettes so give them a try.

Wine

You might not consider wine to be a flavor enhancer, but it truly is. You will see TV chefs using it liberally in beef stock, sauces, or in just about any other dish. It may not surprise you that the French love putting wine in their food. If you ever taste a genuine French Beef Burgundy (the proper term is bourguignon), you will appreciate the liberal use of red wine. C'est magnifique!

Technique Quiz

We are just about halfway through. Let's see how much you've learned from our focus on Technique:

1) What should you always do when buying fruits and vegetables?

a. Feel and observe.

b. Ask the vegetable clerk to decide for you.

c. Avoid anything leafy or green.

d. Take a bite out of them.

2) Why does fish sometimes smell fishy?

a. Because it's fish, duh.

b. Because it begins to decompose after it dies.

c. Because of an organic compound called amine.

d. None of the above.

e. All of the above.

3) Which meat is not graded by the USDA?

a. Chicken

b. Lamb

c. Fish

d. Pork

4) If you want to use pork in spaghetti, what kind is OK?

a. Jimmy Dean's pork sausage

b. Chorizo

c. A slab of fatback

d. Andouille

e. Italian sausage

f. b, d and e only

g. e only

h. b, d or e

5) Which piece of the chicken does not fry well?

a. Thigh

b. Leg

c. Wing

d. Breast

Success

- Following Directions
- Basic How-tos
- Classes & Publications
- Cooking FAQs

"When we no longer have good cooking
in the world, we will have no literature,
nor high and sharp intelligence,
nor friendly gathering, nor social harmony."

— *Marie-Antoine Carême*

Following Directions

By now you are aware that this is not a recipe book, and rightly so because there are more than enough already available to fill the Library of Congress. But since recipes are an integral part of cooking, let's talk about them—the good and the bad.

Recipe Books

You may have noticed that I call them "recipe books" and not "cookbooks." That's because these books, as a rule, do not teach cooking; they simply provide the right mix of ingredients to duplicate a dish. Why do you think cooking shows are so popular? Women (and men) got tired of trying recipes only to end up with the wrong results!

Some recipe books are designed to take you away from the doldrums of everyday cooking and whisk you off to another land where food is as intimate and personal as a romantic relationship. Others whittle cooking down to the bare bones and provide only titles, ingredients and instructions.

I don't like either. That's because I don't need to be carried off to another world, all I really need is enough useful information and instructions to create the dish. In fact, a good recipe book should contain three vital parts for each dish:

1. A recipe that is accurate.

2. Clear instructions that are easy to follow.

3. A final photo showing how the dish will look if created successfully.

That's it! No fancy scenery, no background narrative on the originating country, just the facts.

Inaccurate instructions have ruined many a dish, that's why I make a habit of comparing recipes. Number 2 goes without saying, and the final photo builds confidence that you actually did it right.

Unfortunately, most recipe books do not provide information on the proper utensils, bowls, pots or pans to use, and that is why you are reading this book. Plus, I am also telling you mamas' secrets, which you can't find in any one book anywhere else.

Now that you know what to do, the tools you need and how to use them, it's time to begin the concert. But like any maestro, you must first tune the orchestra.

While you are preparing your meal, you do not want to find yourself running all over the kitchen searching for ingredients or, heaven forbid, trying to measure them, while your recipe is in progress. This situation can lead to all kinds of problems. Recipes are meant to be followed from A to Z with no unscheduled downtime in between.

Here is an example: Let's say you are attempting to make a lemon meringue pie. The lemon filling is resting in the refrigerator and you are in the middle of beating your egg whites for the meringue, when you read in the recipe that you need cream of tartar at this stage of the process. You did not notice it before and you don't have time to go searching for it now. Once you stop beating those eggs, you run the risk of ruining the meringue.

Or imagine you are baking a soufflé. Soufflés must be carefully mixed or they will fall in the oven. You must have all your ingredients at the ready to make a success of this elusive dish. So, in this section, I am going to give you a few tips on how to prevent these kinds of disasters.

Before I break my first egg, shake my first dash of salt or crack open my first box of anything, I read the recipe. Reading it first ensures no surprises later. As you read, consider these things:

The ingredients and their amounts. Do you have any Hungarian Paprika in your pantry? Does the local grocery store carry bok choy?

Whether you will need all the servings it yields. If you don't, calculate how you will cut the recipe in half and write down the new amounts needed before measuring.

What is being asked of you. Do you know what a "translucent" onion looks like? Do you know what "sauté" means and how to do it?

Do you own the particular pot or pan necessary and in the correct size? Some cookware can be substituted, but it's best to determine that in advance. Also make sure your backup pan can take the heat required.

To be prepared for all of the above, let's review each one in depth:

Review the ingredients and their amounts. The worst problem that I experience when I'm cooking a meal is missing items. I'll look in the pantry or cupboard and see that the last drop of something is gone. To avoid running into this difficulty, start paying close attention to the ingredients you use often; make sure you pick up extras every time you see them on sale at the grocery. That is the purpose of "buy one get one free" sales that many grocery stores feature as a pitch to keep their customers coming back. I always keep extra items in a reserved cupboard. Some cooks use the pantry. Maybe your mother or grandmother also had a deep freezer in the garage or a back room where she stored meat and other freezable items. This is one of the signs of a well-prepared cook.

In addition, there may be ingredients you need for a particular recipe that you never heard of before or never found at the local grocery store. Prior to making that recipe, sit down and review what you need. Find out if there is a local farmer's market and visit it well in advance to see what they stock. You may be able to request what you need and come back to retrieve it later when they have it.

Determine whether you will need all the servings it yields. You may need to cut a recipe in half if the servings that it yields are more than you need for your meal. To do this, take a look at all the measurements it requires then get yourself a calculator—unless you can do this in your head—and cut the amounts in half. It's best to write these new amounts down so you do not end up looking at the originals on the recipe. Once written, put them over the original or put the original away until you have all the ingredients measured and in custard dishes.

When reading the instructions, take time to understand what is being asked of you. Recipes sometimes contain terms you do not understand or give explanations of things that may not make sense to you at first reading. This is why it is a good practice to read the recipe aloud to see if there is anything you are being told to do that is not correct. I have come across a few recipes that made absolutely no sense; they either left out a sentence or transposed a few words. Either way, you certainly can't cook a dish when you can't follow the recipe. It's also a good practice to read in advance to be sure you can do what they are asking.

I use a particular technique when tackling a recipe for the first time. I usually first decide that I want to make a particular dish, such as blackberry cobbler, and then I go through all my cookbooks to see if there is a good recipe. I next compare the ones I found to see if the ingredients are the same and the steps are similar. I may go online and find a few more, just in case.

I go through this ritual to ensure that the recipe is accurate. If three cooks say to use something and the fourth one does not, I am inclined to follow the advice of the majority. If I am looking for a particular treatment, such an egg wash and sugar glaze, I may stray from the experts to find one that contains that piece of the recipe. You follow me? Not everyone will cook the same thing the same way, and you want to eventually make that recipe your own.

After all this homework, I make notes on the recipe so I can remember what I did that worked and what did not. For instance, I was making chocolate cupcakes and the recipe called for black coffee. I did not have any, but I did have some Godiva coffee liqueur, which I used. I loved the result and made sure to note that on my recipe.

Regarding unusual terms, here are a few you may see, along with their definitions:

Cream

If you do a lot of baking, you will eventually be asked to perform this task. Creaming is the act of putting butter, or cream cheese, and sugar in a mixer and mashing them together until they are one. Back in the day, cooks used to cream by hand, which is why their arms were so strong. Now we use the standing mixer or hand mixer to do the dirty work. Creaming is usually followed by adding eggs and flour in an alternating fashion. The mixer also does a beautiful job of this, so that all you have to do is pour it into your baking pans. Sweet!

Poach

I rarely poach anything, but this technique is used for eggs and some fish. Poaching allows the food to cook in a water-base so it does not scorch or burn, but cooks inside.

Sauté

This means to cook on the stovetop using medium heat with a little oil. The purpose is to lightly cook or brown. An example of sautéing is cooking garlic, or chopped green peppers, to soften them up before you proceed with the next part of the recipe, such as adding chicken broth, which halts the browning process of sautéing so that you can add ingredients that don't need to be browned or softened.

Sear

This is basically browning the meat on both sides. The heat is usually medium high or a little higher. The goal is to brown not cook, since you will continue to cook the meat using another process, such as baking or simmering.

Simmer

This step is necessary to complete the cooking process, as was mentioned. Simmering is also used for foods such as quinoa or rice. These foods are brought to a boil first, for about a minute, then you put the lid on the saucepan and turn the heat to low. At this point your food is simmering.

Sweat

Sweating is similar to sautéing in that the heat is not very high. The difference is that sweating is just to soften, such as in the case of onions, to get them to the translucent stage, and not to brown.

Translucent

This means clear or see-through. You will be able to tell if onions are translucent from the shine they take on.

Obviously there are other terms you will come across as you try new recipes, especially if you venture into French cooking. The French have their own unique cooking language that once mastered will make you the belle of the kitchen ball. Don't be afraid to try new things.

Do you own the particular pot or pan necessary and in the correct size? This is pretty self-explanatory. If a recipe calls for an aluminum pan and you use a Pyrex dish, expect the results to be different. As mentioned in the Preparation chapter, not all pans are created equal. Also, when baking, size matters. Don't bake your cake in a smaller pan than the recipe calls for or you may see your batter overflowing in the oven.

Cooking Shows

Thank goodness someone invented the cooking show, right? Of course, the Food Network and the Cooking Channel were not the first to get into this game. The very first TV cooking show is up for debate, depending on whether you consider a local show as opposed to a national one as the "first", but regardless, here are a few of the shows that came long before the current crop: *I Love to Eat with James Beard* (1946), *The Galloping Gourmet* (1969), *The Frugal Gourmet* (1973) and *What's Cooking with LaDeva Davis* (1975). All four of these shows aired at local PBS stations.

Cooking shows are great teachers if you can keep up with the host. But they often are not as easy to follow as Queen Latifah makes it look in the movie *Last Holiday* when she cooks along with Emeril Lagasse to make *Poulet Tchoupitoulas* (that recipe is fabulous, by the way). They move way too fast and you don't have time to think about what they just did or why. If you get lost, you can't stop them to ask a question.

Here is my approach. First I just watch the chef walk through the recipe. If I like the results and the process is not too complicated, I go online to download the recipe. Isn't technology wonderful? So I'm not against these shows. On the contrary, I encourage you to watch, learn and try. The more you do this, the less you will need to call your mama!

The only criticism I have of these shows is the lack of basic training. One of the best shows for tips is *Good Eats* with Alton Brown. He at least tries to break it down.

Cooking by sight

This is the one technique that can rarely be taught. Once a person has a few years of consistent cooking under his or her belt, cooking by sight becomes second nature. What this really means is that you are able to determine how much of something is too much and what is not enough. You can put in a pinch of salt, or a dollop of cream and know it's going to be good. But it is not foolproof, as many seasoned cooks will tell you. Sometimes you have an off day and things do not turn out as planned. But in general, because you've done it so many times, you just know.

Most of the women I interviewed have been cooking by sight for years, but that does not mean they will not follow a recipe. Still, once they have created a recipe a few times, they no longer need it again. They are sight cooking. There is no secret to it, and you can do it too with practice and diligence.

So don't feel bad if you cannot cook this way on your first day out. Be kind to yourself and take your time. It will come.

Classes & Publications

Everyone has a certain learning style. Some of us are auditory, and others of us are visual. But many are kinetic. They just need to do it to understand how. For those people, I suggest attending a few cooking classes. They are offered all over the country and are a great way to get some hands-on training in an environment where you can mess up and it's OK.

To find the best ones, contact your local culinary school. They may offer classes for the casual cook, or they may be able to point you in the right direction.

In some cities you can find classes sponsored by Viking, the range manufacturer. The Viking School offers everyday folks a ton of different instructional options: You can learn the basics, such as how to handle kitchen knives or create a complete romantic dinner for that special someone. The schools offer classes every day of the month, to fit just about every schedule. I attended an all-day French cooking class at one of the schools last year. I was in a large kitchen with 12 other newbies, two chefs and several sous chefs running around attending to our needs. We made French bread, cheese soufflés, beef bourguignon and apple tarts. We had a great time. When the cooking was over, we ate the fruits of our labor and went home with some new skills.

The Viking School is usually housed at the same location as their retail stores, so you can peruse their new ranges. They also offer all kinds of kitchen gadgets for sale, as well as a lot of recipe books.

Magazines can be a big help when learning to cook. They are a good resource because they show you the finished product and how to create it. They are preferable to recipe books because they are relatively inexpensive; you don't have to make such a serious commitment as you would with a cookbook. A few of the better ones include *Cooking Light*, *Bon Appetit!* and *Southern Living*. And as I mentioned in the introduction to this book, just about every cooking magazine has an app you can download onto your smartphone or other mobile device.

You can also find good recipes with great pictures in print or online magazines that are not directly connected to food, such as *Good Housekeeping* or *Real Simple*. Even some of the high-end women's magazines contain recipes from time to time. And if you are fortunate, you may find some that dedicate space to cooking tips. I suggest you snatch them up when you see them then put them in an online or paper scrapbook so you can build up your knowledge and share it with friends.

Basic How-tos

*A*fter examining all of the previous information, you are now ready to try some time-tested tips on the basics—things you will likely cook regularly as you embark on your cooking journey. The following basics are explained in detail so you should have no trouble performing them.

Cabbage

Depending upon what you like, there are four basic cabbage types to choose. The familiar green cabbage is used for dishes such as corned beef and cabbage, or it can be simmered with onions as a side. Red cabbage is the purple variety. It is used to give color to coleslaw and salads and is milder than green cabbage. Savoy cabbage is considered the best, but it is not so widely available. It is also milder than green cabbage with wrinkly leaves and a smaller head. Less common varieties are napa, which looks like lettuce, and bok choy, which is used in stir-fried dishes.

Cabbage is fairly easy to cook and in some instances is not cooked at all, such as for coleslaw. To simmer cabbage for a side dish, follow these steps:

1. Get out the cutting board and a large knife.

Note: Be careful to keep your fingers out of the way.

2. Carefully cut the cabbage in half through the core.

3. Now cut each half through its core.

4. Lay each quarter on its side and cut out the core.

Note: The core is too tough to eat so get rid of it.

5. With your fingers folded back out of the way, slice the sections lengthwise, thinly.

6. Take the shredded cabbage and put it in a bowl.

7. Get out a large skillet or sauté pan, adding a little olive oil.

8. Turn the stove burner on medium (not too high and not too low).

9. Once the pan is warm, add the cabbage.

Note: If you use a large head of cabbage you may see it pile up in the pan. Don't be alarmed. Cabbage cooks down to half its size (like collards do). Just let it cook and stir it occasionally. Eventually you will be able to put on the lid.

10. Using a wooden spoon, move the cabbage around so that it gets a little coated with the oil.

11. You may want to add some chicken broth to assist in the cooking process and to prevent burning. I like to add onion ringlets then season it with salt, pepper and onion powder.

12. Put a lid on the cabbage and let it simmer on low.

13. Once the cabbage is soft, it is ready; that can be judged by how you like your cabbage.

Cake Batter

Unlike regular cooking, baking is precise and leaves little room for alteration when it comes to the order of doing things. One of my secrets to great cake batter is really very simple. When combining your dry ingredients—the flour, salt and baking powder—use a hand sifter, like the kind cooks in the 50s and 60s used to use. Sifting is the difference between a light and fluffy cake and one that is not so because if you do not sift, the dry ingredients will not be evenly distributed throughout the cake. One of my cakes tasted like baking soda due to not sifting. This can also happen with pancakes if you do not mix the dry together thoroughly.

After sifting, do not throw the dry and wet ingredients all together at the same time. There are several reasons the dry is mixed separate from the wet before they are combined: First, as already mentioned, the dry ingredients must be evenly distributed, when they hit the wet ingredients they will combine properly. Second, certain ingredients are active and will begin to do their jobs too soon if not combined properly. In addition, you would have to over beat them to get them to combine, which can also yield bad results. Some recipes will ask you to alternate dry and wet ingredients. This technique guarantees better emulsion, resulting in smooth batter.

To determine if a cake is done, at the end of the cooking time, look through the window: does the top look browned? Is it splitting open (in the case of a Bundt cake)? Or does it look wet?

If it still looks like batter, do not open the door. Let it keep cooking. If it is browned and smooth, open the oven and put four fingers over the cake, gently press down. If it springs back it's done. If it is split at the top, that is a good sign as well.

Mashed Potatoes

The first bit of advice is to make sure you buy Russet potatoes. Not all potatoes are good for mashing. Check the package because sometimes it will tell you how to use them. Russets are more floury than waxy and will make fluffy white potatoes. You can also mash red-skinned potatoes, but they are best for roasting. White potatoes are OK too. Avoid using waxy potatoes because they will become sticky and look yellowish due to their starch content.

For a two-person household, you will likely need about four or five medium-sized potatoes. This will depend on how much you eat and how much you both like potatoes.

How you boil your potatoes will depend on whether you want skins in the final result. For instance, some recipes call for red-skinned potatoes and they may tell you not to peel them. If that is fine with you, then you will boil your potatoes without peeling first.

But for regular mashed potatoes, you should clean them under the tap with a bristle brush then peel them with a paring knife or potato peeler. I suggest you peel your potatoes over the garbage disposal so you can easily discard the skins. If you don't have a disposal, use the plastic-bag-in-a-bowl method we discussed in chapter one.

As you are peeling, if you see dark spots on your potatoes, just cut them out. They won't hurt you, but if they go deep and there is pus, throw out the potato and reach for a new one. Also if some of your potatoes look wrinkly and feel malleable, they are also going bad.

Mama's Tip

Don't make mashed potatoes too early or they will get hard when they get cold. Make them just before serving if possible.

There are many methods for mashing; here's mine:

Once your potatoes are peeled and cut in quarters, follow these steps:

1. Get out a stockpot or stainless steel Dutch oven.

Note: If your stockpot has a strainer, use it so that you can easily discard the water after cooking. If not, put a vegetable strainer in the sink to catch any potatoes that may fall out while draining.

2. Fill the pot halfway with water.

Note: The water should just cover the potatoes.

3. Turn the burner on high to get the water to a rolling boil.

4. Gently place your potatoes in the pot, being careful not to splash

the water on yourself.

5. Let the potatoes cook for about 15 minutes then check them by sticking a fork in one. If the fork goes through easily, check another to ensure doneness. If the potato breaks on impact they are good for mashing.

6. Turn off the burner and, using a pair of potholders, take the pot to the sink and pour out the water.

7. Drain the water in the strainer then pour the potatoes back into the pot.

8. Bring the pot back to the stove but do not turn on the heat, season the potatoes with salt and pepper.

9. Now, using a potato masher or a fork, begin breaking up the potatoes.

10. Once they are sufficiently broken up, bring out your hand mixer.

11. Get the milk and butter out of the refrigerator.

12. Add about 2 tablespoons of butter to the potatoes and mix slightly with a wooden spoon.

13. Pour just a little milk into them to get them wet, but do not drown them. About 1/8 cup or less will do. You can add more if you need to during the mixing process.

14. Using the hand mixer, beat the potatoes on a low setting until they begin to look whipped but not thin. If they are too thick, add a

little more milk and beat some more. You want a nice smooth consistency, not watery and not hard.

15. Once done, put the lid on the potatoes and leave them alone until you are ready to serve them. Don't wait too long or they will get hard.

Pan Gravy

Mashed potatoes are not complete without gravy. The trick to good gravy is in the flour or cornstarch paste. You need this paste to thicken the gravy but if it's lumpy your gravy is ruined.

The best gravy is made from pan drippings that result from your oven-baked chicken or turkey. Do not try to make gravy from the pan drippings of anything fried. If you do, you will have oily gravy.

Some cooks prefer to use flour as a base for gravy, but I find that cornstarch works best because it does not get lumpy like flour and it doesn't leave a taste. Even the best cooks can botch flour-based gravy. Cornstarch is pretty much foolproof.

If after seasoning the gravy you find that your pan drippings are not that flavorful, you can add a few drops of **Kitchen Bouquet Browning and Seasoning Sauce**. This sauce has been around for years and is available in the condiments aisle at the grocery. It adds not only great flavor but also color so your gravy does not look white when you wanted it brown. Don't overdo this sauce; a little goes a long way.

1. Remove the meat from the roaster. Move the roaster to the stove and heat the drippings over two burners.

2. Scrape any bits from the bottom of the pan and mix them in.

3. Once this is hot, stir in about 2 cups of store bought chicken or turkey broth and continue to heat.

4. In a small bowl, add about 1 tablespoon of cornstarch. If you prefer flour about a heaping fork is enough for starters.

5. Now, get a 1/8 measuring cup and use it to remove some of the hot broth. Pour half of it in the bowl with the flour or cornstarch. You want to create a thin paste. Stir. Again, if you use flour, make sure there are no lumps present.

6. Pour the paste into the pan drippings and broth on the stove and stir until all the white disappears.

7. As you stir, you should notice the liquid get thicker.

8. If you want the gravy darker, add in a drop or two of the Kitchen Bouquet.

9. Let this continue to heat through. If it is still not thick enough for you, repeat steps 4 through 6, using less paste.

10. Salt and pepper your gravy to taste. If you feel you need more pan drippings, add an extra tablespoon at a time until you are happy with the taste.

Meringue

Meringue is one of my favorite things to make because it's fun and is used to top my favorite dessert: lemon meringue pie.

Making meringue requires a good eye and a good mixer. The ingredients you need to set out in advance are cream of tartar and sugar. Measure both and have them at the ready *before* you begin beating the egg whites. The amount of each will vary depending on how much you are making and whether you use fresh farm eggs or pasteurized (carton) eggs.

I use an electric hand mixer for my meringue, but you can also use a standing mixer. I would suggest you use the standing mixer your first time out so that the beating remains continuous. If you stop beating meringue once the process starts, you will mess it up. Additionally, this is another one of those recipes where you cannot put all the ingredients in at the same time, so don't do it!

> ### Mama's Tip
>
> If you are making hot filling, such as lemon, you will want to make the meringue before the filling. Why? Because the filling should still be hot when you top it with the meringue; this will help it to set at the base, resulting in a more stable meringue.

1. First, open your oven and put the rack in the middle, then preheat it to the required temperature. If you are

making only meringue for a no-bake pie, set it at 325 degrees just to brown the meringue (about 15 minutes or so).

2. Get out two custard bowls so you can separate your eggs. Cold eggs separate better, so do this right out of the refrigerator. This meringue recipe only uses 3 egg whites. If you want more meringue, use 4 eggs but do not increase the amount of cream of tartar.

3. After separating, let the whites sit for about 20 minutes to allow them to get to room temperature; they whip up better if you wait.

4. Get out a larger bowl, preferably steel, that is clean and free of fat. Any fat will react with the meringue and ruin the results. Do not use plastic or copper bowls for meringue.

5. Pour in the egg whites and begin beating them at a brisk setting, such as 4 for the standing mixer and 2 or 3 for a hand mixer; basically the middle setting.

6. They will begin to look foamy. This is good. Keep beating.

7. Add a ¼ teaspoon cream of tartar for pasteurized eggs. For fresh eggs, use 1/8 teaspoon. Keep beating.

8. Now add 2 tablespoons of sugar. Keep beating.

9. Soon your meringue will take on a shine and have stiff peaks that remain when you pull the beater out of the bowl. If they do not stand up on their own, keep beating.

10. If you have not already done so, pour the filling in a prepared pie

shell (some shells should be pre-baked so check your recipe).

11. Dollop the meringue onto the pie using a plastic spatula, the kind used for frosting.

12. Lightly but evenly spread the meringue to the edges of the pie, being careful not to disturb the filling. Do not dig into the meringue!

13. You can make peaks on the meringue by lightly tapping the spatula up and down on the surface.

14. Put that puppy in the oven!

Note: I have tried using substitute egg whites for my meringue and they do not form the stiffness you will need; therefore, I would advise against them so your meringue does not go south.

Rice

Before we get into how to cook rice, let me explain the different types. Plain white (long-grain) rice is neutral in flavor and is best for rice pilaf. Short-grain rice is thicker than long-grain and sticks together when cooked. It is best for sushi or rice pudding. Brown rice still contains the bran, so it has a shorter shelf life. It also requires more time to cook than white rice, about 45 minutes total, but always read the directions on the package to be sure. Aromatic rice comes as white or brown and has a flavor similar to roasted nuts or popcorn.

A few of the most common rice types are listed below:

Jasmine—Aromatic, soft, brown or white.

Basmati—Aromatic, long-grain, slender.

Brown—Whole grain with the hull removed.

Wild—Usually combined with long-grain rice, it is a dark, aquatic grass seed and so not technically rice.

Yellow—Considered a rice mix because it is rice with seasonings added.

Rice can be a tragic dish if you do not cook it properly. Not enough cooking time will make it watery and not enough water will make it crunchy. You want to avoid both. Before we begin, here are the ground rules: All rice is not created equal, meaning make your choices carefully. If the box says "quick cooking" then my method will not work. For that rice, follow the directions on the box. But if you are cooking natural, long-grain, white rice, this is the method for you:

1. Measure one cup of rice and pour it into a 2-quart saucepan.

2. Pour in 2 cups of water.

Note: For every cup of rice, you need two cups of water.

3. Turn the burner on medium-high.

4. Bring the rice and water to a rolling boil. Once boiling, let it do so for about one minute.

Note: Some may tell you not to put the rice in the water until it has boiled. That method works too.

5. Now turn down the burner to a low simmer, place the lid on the

saucepan and cook for about 25 minutes. You will have to get a feel for the time as you get more proficient.

6. After the allotted time has elapsed, remove the saucepan from the burner and set it on a trivet. Remove the lid and place a clean, folded dishtowel over the pan. Replace the lid and gently press down.

Note: Do not try to put the towel over the saucepan until you have removed it from the stove. We don't want a fire; we want tasty rice.

7. Allow the towel to absorb the remaining water for 15 minutes.

8. Remove the lid and towel.

At this point, your rice should be well cooked and fluffy. If you wish, add a pat of butter (half a tablespoon) then replace the lid until ready to serve.

Roux

A roux is normally called for as a base in Cajun or French recipes and is a fairly long process because waiting for it to turn just the right shade of brown takes time. The key is in the stirring, and stirring and stirring. Get the point? Well then here goes:

1. Get out one half stick of butter (1/8 lb.) then measure 1/2 cup of flour, and ¼ cup of peanut oil.

2. Place a sauté pan on the burner and turn the heat to medium-high.

3. Melt the butter and the oil and then, with a wooden spoon, stir

in the flour, making sure it is well blended.

4.   Now you just stir it until it turns a dark caramel color, which can take up to 20 minutes so don't make any plans to do anything else until this is done. And don't burn it or it will lose its flavor.

Zucchini (or squash)

Squash is one of the easiest vegetables to prepare, and it doesn't take much to make it taste great. Whether you choose yellow or green, you can't go wrong with it as a complementary side dish.

Note: Don't prepare this vegetable until almost everything else is ready; it could get too soft if it has to sit.

1.   Wash the skin with a vegetable brush and water.

2.   Get out a small cutting board and a steak or paring knife (squash is easy to cut so you don't need the heavy artillery).

3.   Slice it to the desired width suitable for eating, such as you would a cucumber, then put the slices in a plastic bowl.

4.   Get out a small sauté or frying pan and add a little olive oil. About a tablespoon or two should do it.

5.   Turn the burner on medium.

6.   While the squash is still in the bowl, sprinkle some adobo seasoning on the slices (you can find adobo in the ethnic food aisle at the grocer). You don't need anything else. Mix the squash to ensure good

coverage.

7. Dump the slices into the fryer and, using a wooden spatula or spoon, begin sautéing the slices. Just keep moving them around the pan, allowing them to flip over and over until they are fairly soft but not wilted.

8. Remove the slices from the pan and place them on a plate or in a bowl. Delicious!

Success Quiz

Now that we have come to the end of the Success chapter, as usual, let's review what you've learned.

1) What three things should a good recipe book contain? (choose 3)

a. An accurate recipe.

b. Photos of the final result.

c. Clear instructions.

d. Lots of narrative about life in Tuscany.

2) What four things should you consider when reviewing a new recipe? (choose 4)

a. The types of ingredients and the amounts.

b. If you can skimp on some of the ingredients.

c. If you need all the servings it yields.

d. If you have all the items you will need.

e. If the recipe is American or European.

f. If you understand what to do.

g. If you feel like cooking today.

3) **Match the term on the left with the correct definition on the right.**

TERM	DEFINITION
1. Translucent	a. To beat briskly by hand
2. Cream	b. Slow cooking
3. Saute	c. Clear or see-through
4. Simmer	d. Combining two or three items into a silky mass
5. Poach	e. Browning over low heat
6. Whisk	f. Water-based cooking approach

4) **What is the best method for freezing meat?**

a. Throw it in the freezer in its original packaging.

b. Take it out of the package and seal it in an airtight freezer bag.

c. Wrap it in cellophane.

d. Put it in Mama's deep freezer.

e. Place it in a brown paper bag.

5) Match the instruction on the right with the correct item on the left.

ITEM	INSTRUCTION
1. Rice	a. Don't leave this out overnight or it will stink up the whole house.
2. Fish	b. For the best taste, cook this until it's soft.
3. Lamb	c. There are several cooking methods for this depending on what type it is.
4. Flour	d. Never cook anything else in the same oil used for cooking this.
5.Cabbage	e. Use two parts water with every one part of this.
6. Potato	f. Don't re-use this item for anything after it has been used once.

Cooking FAQs

As I was doing research for this book, many people began asking questions they've been burning to get an answer to about basic cooking and food preparation. Here are some of those questions. I hope something in this list can help you too.

Q: *How many types of flour are there and what are their uses?*

A: There are five basic flour types: all-purpose, self-rising, bread, cake and whole wheat. There are others you will rarely use and I will discuss them later.

- *All-purpose* is the most widely available flour; less expensive than cake and bread flour. It is also called enriched flour because iron and vitamins are added to it.

- *Self-rising* is just all-purpose flour with ½ teaspoon of salt and 1½ teaspoons of baking powder added per cup. So if you use this flour to bake, reduce the salt and baking powder in your recipe by these amounts. Self-rising flour costs about the same as all-purpose.

- *Bread flour* has more gluten, so it's best for making yeast breads. It is more expensive than regular flour.

- *Cake flour* makes your pastries more delicate because it is a finer grind. It has less protein than bread flour but more starch. Cake flour is more expensive than regular flour.

Note: If you use all-purpose flour but want the consistency of cake flour, just remove two tablespoons of the flour per cup and replace that with two tablespoons of cornstarch.

• *Whole wheat flour* contains less gluten due to the bran; it makes a heavier bread. It is more expensive than regular flour.

 Less common types of flour are pastry flour (which is a cross between all-purpose and cake flour); semolina and durum, both used for making pasta; gluten, which has a high-protein content; and graham, which is a coarsely ground whole-wheat type.

Q: *Do all cooking oils burn at the same temperature?*

A: Actually, I think you are asking about the "smoke point"; the higher the smoke point the less likely the oil will smoke at high temps. From all the books I've read, this depends on several things, such as the color of the oil, the type of oil and how long it's been on the burner. If the oil is old, meaning it has been used, the smoke point is reduced. Refined oil has a higher smoke point than non-refined. And vegetable oil usually has a higher smoke point than animal fat.

For more on smoke points, search the Internet with the keywords "smoke point." You will find a chart listing all the oils and their heating limits.

Q: *Do greens have to be cooked for hours to taste good?*

A: Great question and the answer is no. In fact, I prefer to sauté my greens in an anodized skillet and then add a little chicken broth to steam them the rest of the way. I adapted my method from a Chef G. Garvin recipe. The cooking time is about 35 minutes. You should check him out at **www.chefgarvin.com**.

Q: *I saw a butternut squash at the grocery and wondered how to cook it. Can you help?*

A: I recently made soup with that squash for my husband. First, be aware that this squash is hard to cut. You need strong arms or someone with strong arms to assist. I wore myself out cutting it up. I suggest buying a couple of small ones instead. That said, once it is sliced lengthwise, scoop out all the seeds and that other "stuff" and discard. Then you can skin it with a paring knife. Next, cut it into cubes and put the cubes in a bowl. Drizzle them with olive oil and shake on some salt. Pour them onto a baking sheet and bake them until toasted around the edges. Stick a fork into one and if it goes through they are done. You can either eat them as is or put them in a food processor to make soup. There are lots of easy butternut squash soup recipes out there, so experiment!

Q: *What are capers and how are they used?*

A: Capers come from the caper bush and are the flowering bud of the plant; they look dark and green after being sun-dried and brined in vinegar. They are used to enhance the flavor of foods and are usually found in Salad Nicoise, which is a French salad made with tuna and boiled eggs, among other things. Some use anchovies and capers interchangeably. Although they are both salty, they do not taste the same. Capers are good with seafood and pasta dishes.

Q: *How can you tell when spaghetti is really done?*

A: Hmm. The doneness of spaghetti depends on how you like it. Boil it until the yellow is faded, then take a set of tongs and pull out a strand. Place it on a plate to cool then eat it. If it's too chewy, keep cooking it. Some call that al dente and they prefer it, but if you don't, keep cooking. On the other hand, if it's kind of mushy and soft, you may have overcooked it. You want to shoot for something between chewy and soft. One other tip about spaghetti: after you drain the pasta, don't pour the sauce on it right after it's cooked. Keep the two separate until they get on the plate. That way, you don't waste pasta by mixing it prematurely with the sauce and discovering you made too much pasta and not enough sauce.

Q: *How can I season baked chicken to make it taste good every time?*

A: Baking chicken is a great alternative to frying if you are trying to cut back on your fat intake. But sometimes it just doesn't taste as good. You can remedy that by using a rub prior to baking. You can develop your own mix of seasonings or use this spicy combo.

Put your chicken parts (I recommend boneless thighs) in a big bowl and then mix these spices together in a smaller bowl with a ½ cup of olive oil:

- 1T Oregano
- 1T Onion powder
- 1T Dried thyme
- 2T Garlic powder
- 1T Cayenne pepper
- 2T Salt
- 1T Pepper
- 2T Paprika

Put on some disposable latex cooking gloves and rub the mix all over every piece of chicken. Throw away the gloves. Now heat up a fryer and brown the pieces. After they are browned, place them in a pot that is oven safe, such as a Staub or Lodge Dutch oven, and bake at 350 degrees for 30 minutes. I would suggest keeping the lid on for moister meat.

Q: *I bought some fresh vegetables from the farmer's market and once I got them home I wasn't sure how to begin. What do I do to prepare things like asparagus, string beans or greens for cooking?*

A: Wow, that's a loaded question that could be answered several ways, but I think you want to know how to clean them and prep them for cooking. If so, one of the first things you should do actually starts at the farmer's market (or grocery store). When choosing fresh vegetables, notice how they look. Are they bruised? Are the leaves wilted? If it is a green vegetable, are any parts of it brown? Pick up a few and feel them. Are they soft when they should be firm? If you are really unsure about all this, ask the produce person to assist you.

Step two comes once you get them home. Wash them. You may even want to scrub the skin with a vegetable brush; items such as collard greens can harbor dirt and bugs in the vein area of the leaves. Just be sure everything is rinsed sufficiently. Dry them with paper towels.

What I like to do next is cut off the ends. If I am buying heads, such as lettuce and cabbage, I remove the outer leaves and trash them. If I am working with fresh green beans, I cut off both ends and snap them in half. I learned that as a youngster. During the summer I would visit my uncle and aunt's farm, and we passed the hours on the porch shucking corn and snapping green beans.

As a rule, I like to cut off the ends of asparagus, squash, green onions or any other veggie with an end on it. It's like discarding the end of a loaf of bread; you just don't want it. The only exception is the onion. In that case, I cut off one end and keep the core so that I can use it to keep all the slices together. From there, I peel off the skin, then cut the onion in half then slice vertically from the core. After that I cut horizontally. When I am done I throw away the core.

Q: *I bought some chicken, threw it in the freezer then thawed it out for cooking a few days later. But my husband and I ended up going out to eat so I put the chicken back in the freezer. Is that OK?*

A: Can I assume that you thawed it out in the refrigerator? If so then yes. But if you set it out on the counter to thaw, you are really in trouble. Never do this! It will get warm on the counter and attract bacteria. Meats and fish should always be thawed in the refrigerator or by some other safe method, such as running cold water over the package or setting the package in a sink with some cold water. If you are thawing out shrimp, you can open the package and place the frozen shrimp in a colander. Then set that in the sink and let cold water run over until it thaws.

Q: *I made meatloaf and it turned out really dry. I used ground beef and some sausage, so what did I do wrong?*

A: Not having seen your meatloaf, it's kind of hard to tell, but I have a sneaking suspicion you used lean hamburger. Meatloaf gets its moistness from the fat in the meat, and it needs that fat because you are adding breadcrumbs to it; bread soaks up any liquid it finds. Next time, choose regular ground beef that is less than 80% lean. I would avoid ground chuck and sirloin. Ground turkey or chicken can be substituted, but I have never been satisfied with anything but regular ground beef.

Q: *I was making a dish from a recipe and it called for buttermilk. I didn't have any and my neighbor said to use regular milk and lemon juice. Is that true?*

A: Your neighbor is correct. But you can also use vinegar or cream of tartar to accomplish this. If you go the liquid route, it's one tablespoon of lemon juice or vinegar per cup of whole milk. If you use cream of tartar it's ¾ of a tablespoon per cup of milk. The milk should curdle almost immediately, making it the same as buttermilk. Once the mixture begins to curdle, stir it then let it sit for about 15 minutes. Adding lemon juice to other types of milk may not taste the same. I suggest whole milk since the butterfat is still in it. Now go call your neighbor and apologize for doubting her. And get some more tips while you're at it; she's probably a great cook.

Q: *Every time I fry chicken, it burns. I've tried turning the fire down, but then it doesn't cook inside. What am I doing wrong?*

A: Good fried chicken takes time to master. You not only have to use the right combination of seasoning, but everything has to be correct, right down to the type of oil you use. One of the first tricks I learned about fried chicken had to do with the flour. I use a plastic bag to shake the chicken in a mixture of flour, salt, pepper and paprika. The paprika gives it a nice color.

The key is to shake off most of the flour before you put it in the pan (I do not coat my chicken with any kind of liquid bath). If too much flour gets in the oil, it will burn, taking your chicken along for the ride. You may also want to pay attention to how long you are cooking it as well as the heat level. The oil I use is commonly known as lard (the white Crisco in a can). It may not be healthy, but I love the taste. Of course, you can substitute using peanut, vegetable or any oil with a high smoke point. But don't use olive oil.

If you have a gas stove, the heat should be on medium high the entire cooking time. Make sure the oil is hot before adding the chicken and don't put in too many pieces. Give it some room to cook. If you overcrowd the pan, the temperature will not stay as hot as it needs to do the job right.

It should take about 15 minutes on each side to cook the chicken. The best way to get good chicken is to not rush it. Don't watch it constantly, just let that 15 minutes go by while you do something else. After a few experiences cooking chicken, you will get the hang of it and start experimenting with seasonings and coatings.

Q: *I have begun using European style butter instead of sticks. How do I measure it when the recipe calls for a stick of butter?*

A: European butter is usually sold by the half pound (8 oz.) while butter in the states is sold by the pound (16 oz.), but in sticks. That means each of the four sticks in the box weigh a quarter pound (4 oz.), which equates to half the amount of your European butter. Incidentally, the package of European butter should also contain measurements for converting to sticks.

Q: *What is the difference between half & half, whipping cream and heavy whipping cream?*

A: A rule of thumb to remember is the more fat, the thicker the cream. This basically means that if you want a cream that stands up to whipping, get one with lots of fat. Of the three you mention, the heavy whipping cream would contain the most fat. Half & half contains the least amount of fat, and that is why it is best for beverages. Below is a chart with the fat content of each:

CREAM TYPE	FAT CONTENT
Half & half	12%
Whipping cream	35%
Heavy whipping cream	38%

Q: *Does altitude make a difference when following a baking recipe? I live in Colorado, home of the Mile High City.*

A: I've heard a lot of debate about the low-air pressure/high-altitude mix that sometimes ruins recipes. My advice is to try the recipe first to see if it turns out OK. If not, you may want to make some adjustments. For instance, if you live at a level of 5,000 feet or higher, one teaspoon of baking powder will actually equate to 20% more volume. But the bottom line is that everything depends on where you are and how high the elevation; again, experimenting will be the only way to be sure. Once you've tested out a few of your favorite recipes, be sure to write down what worked and what did not.

The chart on the following page should assist you in making the right temperature choices when baking at higher altitudes. The chart is courtesy of King Arthur Flour and seems to be a good starting point.

WHAT TO CHANGE	HOW TO CHANGE IT	WHY
Oven temperature	Increase by 15° to 25°F; use the lower increase when making chocolate or delicate cakes.	Because leavening and evaporation proceed more quickly, the idea is to use a higher temperature to "set" the structure of baked goods before they over expand and dry out.
Baking time	Decrease by 5 to 8 minutes per every 30 minutes of baking time.	Baking at higher temperatures means products are done sooner.
Sugar	Decrease by 1 tablespoon per cup.	Increased evaporation also increases concentration of sugar, which can weaken the structure of what you're baking.
Liquid	Increase by 1 to 2 tablespoons at 3,000 feet. Increase by 1 1/2 teaspoons for each additional 1,000 feet. You can also use extra eggs as part of this liquid, depending on the recipe.	Extra liquid keeps products from drying out at higher temperatures and evaporation rates.
Flour	At 3,500 feet, add one more tablespoon per recipe. For each additional 1,500 feet, add one more tablespoon.	In some recipes, flour with a higher protein content may yield better results. Additional flour helps to strengthen the structure of baked goods.

Reprinted with permission courtesy of kingflour.com

Appendix

Here are the answers from the section quizzes. Hope you did well!

Preparation Quiz Answers

1. Before you start to cook, what is the most important thing to do?

Answer: c

2. What are the **three** reasons for washing your hands before you begin food preparation?

Answers: a, e and f. If you chose d you still get credit for this answer!

3. What is the best thing to do with your hair before cooking?

Answers: b or c. You could shave your head so c is acceptable, but the real answer is b.

4. What should you do to maintain a clean atmosphere throughout the cooking process?

Answer: b. Using the plastic bag and bowl makes clean up easy and mess-free.

5. Which two below should you use to sanitize a cutting board?

Answer: a. Vinegar and water is the best combination and the only correct choice on the list.

Organization Quiz Answers

1. Which cookware should you avoid if you or a dinner guest is highly sensitive to nickel?

Answer: d. Stainless steel contains 8% or 10% nickel, depending on which type you purchase.

2. According to the makers of Pyrex, what should you never do with this cookware when it is hot?

Answer: e. According to World Kitchen, maker of Pyrex, you should never perform any of the actions listed.

3. What kind of oil should NOT be used in a wok?

Answer: g. Either unrefined oils or peanut. Check the smoke point chart when making your choice.

4. How can you tell when oil is hot enough for cooking?

Answer: b. Never throw water in oil or stick your finger in it to test the heat.

5. What are the two **best** utensils to use in any cookware?

Answer: c. Plastic can melt and metal cannot be used on non-stick surfaces.

Technique Quiz Answers

1. What should you always do when buying fruits and vegetables?

Answer: a. The best method is to feel the item and observe whether it has the right color and texture associated with freshness and ripeness.

2. Why does fish sometimes smell fishy?

Answer: e. Yes, fish is fishy because it's fish; when it decomposes it produces amines that cause the stinky smell. Remember that lemon juice is your counter attack, so use it!

3. Which meat is **not** graded by the USDA?

Answer: d. Fish is not a meat.

4. If you want to use pork in spaghetti, what kind is OK?

Answer: h. You can use any of the three in answer h, just don't use JD's or that fatback.

5. Which piece of the chicken does not fry well?

Answer: d. Breasts don't fry well and are best cooked in the oven.

Success Quiz Answers

1. What three things should a good recipe book contain?

Answer: a, b and c. For the new cook, these are essential to success. Once you get comfortable in the kitchen, a trip to Tuscany might be just the ticket!

2. What **four** things should you consider when reviewing a new recipe?

Answers: a, c, d and f. I might accept g, but we ALWAYS feel like cooking, right???

3. Match the term on the left with the correct definition on the right.

Answers: 1c, 2d, 3e, 4b, 5f, 6a.

4. What is the *best* method for freezing meat?

Answer: b. This is the best method, but I will reluctantly accept answer a.

5. Match the instruction on the right with the correct item on the left.

Answers: 1e, 2d, 3a, 4f, 5b, 6c.

DRY MEASURE	EQUIVALENT
1/8 teaspoon	Dash
3 teaspoons	1 Tablespoon
1/8 cup	2 Tablespoons
¼ cup	4 Tablespoons
1/3 cup	5 Tablespoons
½ cup	8 Tablespoons
¾ cup	12 Tablespoons
1 cup	16 Tablespoons
1 pound (lb.)	16 ounces

LIQUID MEASURE	EQUIVALENT
8 fluid ounces (oz.)	1 cup
1 pint	2 cups (16 fluid ounces)
1 quart	2 pints (4 cups)
1 gallon	4 quarts (16 cups)

US MEASURE	METRIC CONVERSION
1/5 teaspoon	1 milliliter (ml)
1 teaspoon	5 ml
1 Tablespoon	15 ml
1 fluid ounce	30 ml
1/5 cup	50 ml
1 cup	240 ml
2 cups (1 pint)	470 ml
4 cups (1 quart)	.95 liter
4 quarts (1 gallon)	3.8 liters
1 ounce	28 grams
1 pound	454 grams

Oven Temperature Conversions

FAHRENHEIT	CELSIUS
275 degrees	140 degrees
300 degrees	150 degrees
325 degrees	165 degrees
350 degrees	180 degrees
375 degrees	190 degrees
400 degrees	200 degrees
425 degrees	220 degrees
450 degrees	230 degrees
475 degrees	240 degrees

Baking Pan Size Conversions

INCHES	CENTIMETERS
9 x 13	22 x 33
8 x 8	20 x 20
9 x 5	23 x 12
10 inch	25 centimeters
9 inch	22 centimeters

Index